GIRL GROUP CONFIDENTIAL

GIRL GROUP CONFIDENTIAL

The Ultimate Guide to Starting, Running, and Enjoying
Your Own Women's Group

Jennifer Worick

STC Paperbacks
Stewart, Tabori & Chang / New York

Cover design by Margie Miller
Illustration by Kerrie Hess/Arts Counsel Inc.
Editor: Marisa Bulzone
Book design by Amanda Wilson
Production Manager: Kim Tyner

Library of Congress Cataloging-in-Publication Data:
  Worick, Jennifer.
  Girl group confidential : the ultimate guide to starting, running,
and enjoying your own women's group / Jennifer Worick.
  p. cm.
  Includes Index
        ISBN 1-58479-479-8
  1. Women--Societies and clubs--Handbooks, manuals, etc. 2.
Women--Social networks--Handbooks, manuals, etc. I. Title.
  HQ1885.W67 2006
  369.068--dc22   2005030866

Published in 2006 by Stewart, Tabori & Chang
An imprint of Harry N. Abrams, Inc.

The text of this book was composed in Priori and Cochin

Printed and bound in the United States of America
10 9 8 7 6 5 4 3 2 1

harry n. abrams, inc.
a subsidiary of La Martinière Groupe
115 West 18th Street
New York, NY 10011
www.hnabooks.com

DEDICATION

To my best friend, Alison Rooney. Between the two of us, we have
a writer's group, knitting circle, financial club, book club, movie night,
gambling group, cooking club, and workout support group.
Thank you for your multifaceted and ever-evolving friendship.

ACKNOWLEDGMENTS

I pledge my undying gratitude to the women who shared their stories and girl groups with me throughout the process of writing this book, namely Maria Young (I love you, Maria); Donna Howard (I love you, friend); Debra Lande; Carol Hamlin; e Bond; Jo Wharton; Kathy Patrick; Sherry Petrie; Callie Crossley, Karen Holmes Ward, Gert Cowan, and all of the Divas Uncorked; Zoe Alexander, Jennifer Ashare, and of all the Divas Who Dine; and Liesa Goins. Thanks also to my girl group hero and foreword writer, Cameron Tuttle, who continually demonstrates that you can use your girl power for bad as well as good. I must also thank a couple of men—after all, they do help make the world go round: Jared Von Arx, who generously shared his lethal punch recipe, and my accountant, Peter Jones, who was an invaluable resource.

And I have to give a shout out to my own girl group: Alison (duh!), Mary Mausheen McGuire Ruggiero, Sacha Adorno, Caroline Tiger, Melissa Wagner, Alicia Freile, Kerry Colburn, Kerry Sturgill, Lynn Rosen, Danielle Burgio, Ann Wilson, Laurel Rivers, Erin Wickersham, Jennifer Schaefer, Jennifer Brunn, Nancy Armstrong, Makaylia Roberts, and Mindy Brown. Thanks for your professional and personal support throughout the years.

Finally, thanks to my very patient and wise editor, Marisa Bulzone, without whom I could never have kept my sanity.

CONTENTS

10   Foreword

13   Introduction: The Female Circle of Support

21   Chapter 1: Getting Your Girl Game On

37   Chapter 2: Assembling the Group

47   Chapter 3: The Rule Book

65   Chapter 4: Hosting

89   Chapter 5: Policing the Ranks

105 Chapter 6: Staying Motivated

121 Chapter 7: Growing Pains & Gains

149 Chapter 8: The Groups

Financial Club ■ Book Club ■ Culture Club ■ Career Club ■ Gaming Group ■ Craft Circle ■ Interest Club ■ Sporting Club ■ Activist or Emotional Support Group ■ Spiritual Gathering ■ Spa Party

167 Resources

173 Index

Let's be honest. Does the world really need one more book telling grown-up girls what to do and how to do it better? Yes! *Girl Group Confidential* serves up all the dishy details to help you organize and nurture a successful girl group—whatever your interests. I love this book. It's not only informative and fun, it's a celebration of what women do best—come together to share their energy, smarts, insights, and passions. And that's what a girl group is all about.

But wait. Who needs to organize a club or an official group just to get together with your girl friends? You do, baby. Sure, you can always go shopping with your best girls and meet on the fly for coffee or cocktails. But a scheduled girl group is different. There is something special and even sacred about taking the time to gather around a shared interest, beloved activity, or master plan. Making that commitment shows that you value yourself and your friends enough to carve time out of your busy lives. And a girl group is the perfect way to see friends without the liability of a hangover, crazy caffeine buzz, or mounting credit card debt.

Most of the things you might do in a girl group you certainly could do alone. But that's the problem—you'd be alone. It's so much more fun to gather as a group and turn "me time" into "we time." You not only benefit from others' ideas, perspectives, and knowledge, you also get to experience that powerful exchange of female energy and support. The best girl groups create a safe space where you can feel free to let it all hang out, be really silly, smart, crazy, fabulous—or all of the above.

These days, the world can seem too big and happen way too fast. It's easy to feel like an outsider at work, watching the news, sitting in traffic, even at home with your own family. A well-designed and managed girl group gives you and every member the feeling of being an insider. Why? Because you are. You get to tailor the group to fit your needs and wants. You determine your group's focus and size as well as the rules and regulations. Do you want to think more, drink more, or knit more? Are you interested in growing your portfolio, or shrinking your butt? Want to see more plays or play more poker? Do you want to hang with old friends or get to know new friends? Whatever type of group sounds fun, you've got the power to make it happen.

I'm not just saying this because I read it in some book. I've experienced that power at many bad-girl gatherings over the years. Currently, I am in a Show-and-Tell group in San Francisco. It's an eclectic bunch of interesting women—and the ideal post-grad-school/pre-senility way to get together with friends and stimulate a few brain cells. The group's founder Deborah Pardes had a brilliantly simple idea to transform the classic elementary school activity into an evening of light edification, perfect for busy women with tired brains. I have had the opportunity to show my collection of heart-shaped beach stones (which before had never made it out of my lingerie drawer) as well as the rather gruesome X-rays of my fractured wrist, featuring five metal pins. (Ouch!) I have learned about TIG welding, the poaching of elephants in Africa, what causes fog, the subtle differences between Greek and Spanish olives, and a few other things I probably shouldn't mention. Once a month we get together over a potluck dinner to learn a bit and end up laughing a lot, feeling enriched, and discovering things about one another that deepen our friendship.

With a little planning and organization, I'm sure your girl gatherings will have the same effect. Whether you're looking to start a small group, a big club, or a social revolution, this book will help you do it with style. Enjoy!

—Cameron Tuttle
Author, *The Bad Girl's Guides*

The Female Circle of Support

"The power of women's voices is just so immense, and when women come together, things move." So says Jo Wharton, a member and founder of several women's groups.

Women have always forged unique bonds with one another. These relationships support, they educate, they encourage, and they inspire.

I certainly can't get along without my circles of female love. There's my knitting circle, where I create and gossip. There's also my monthly poker night, where I gamble and gossip. I had to let my *Sex and the City* weekly dinners go gently into that good night.

I wasn't happy about it.

So while I am searching for another gathering to fill the gap left in my life and social calendar, I notice that women everywhere are gathering more and more frequently, often in organized clubs or groups. Poker nights are not just for the boys. My girlfriends and I gather every few weeks for a night of Texas hold 'em, drinks, and a lot of socializing. Knitting and crochet continue to gain in popularity, and consequently, stitch 'n' bitch nights are joining long-established knitting circles as opportunities for women to come together, create and bond. Bible-study groups, mommy support groups, environmental action clubs, cycling clubs, spa parties, and all types of girl gatherings in between are happening far and wide.

Kathy Patrick, the founder of the nationally franchised Pulpwood Queens book clubs, explained the growing number of girl groups this way: "As women's lives become busy and complicated, it's harder to find time to relax or pursue interests of our own. Attending a group legitimizes your downtime and makes it OK to leave the kids with your husband for a few hours, in a way that doing something by yourself can't."

She sees female gatherings as a necessary tradition that women have enjoyed in some form or another throughout the generations. "Many of our mothers were stay-at-home moms but carved out time to have bridge club or something similar," Kathy says. "Our generation doesn't have that time anymore. If you do take time by yourself, you are considered selfish. But if you are taking off to be with your book club to discuss books, it gives you license to have a good time with girlfriends and decompress. If you learn something, so much the better."

But as much as I'd like to think everything is sweetness and light, problems do crop up. One member may be consistently MIA, or the group may get too big for a living room to accommodate.

That's where *Girl Group Confidential* comes in.

This informal handbook will guide women who are toying with the idea of starting up a group of their own. It will cover the nuts and bolts, like how often to meet, how to control the group size, and even how to disinvite a member (i.e., kicking someone out of the clubhouse). Depending on the type of group or club, you will have different needs and structures. For example, if you are assembling an investment club, rules and guidelines will be important, and roles and responsibilities for members will be key. In contrast, if you are hosting a movie night, the mood will be more laid-back; holding each member to a strict code of conduct won't be necessary. Size matters, as you well know. If you have a small, cozy group of friends, a thick manual will just seem silly, but you will still benefit from laying down a few ground rules at the outset. You'll find troubleshooting tips and advice that will apply to the various groups profiled here, as well as to other burgeoning clubs. No matter what group you belong to or want to belong to, *Girl Group Confidential* will be an invaluable resource.

And if you don't belong to a group yet, it's time to remedy that. Spending time with other women is just plain fun! There's nothing else like it. It feeds the soul and is a vital part of our experience. *Girl Group Confidential* will show women how to optimize female gatherings and make the experience rich and rewarding. Take it from Donna Howard, who is part of a dinner group in Michigan, called Knock Three Times (representing how often the table is rapped when a "take to the grave" secret is revealed). "Having this dinner meeting helps push me beyond my mom persona. I'm a *person*, not just a role. We are all trying to find a balance that works best for us, and once you have children, a husband, and other obligations, it can get complicated to balance everything out. Getting together with my girlfriends reminds me that I am someone else besides a mother."

But why start a group at all, when you can just get together with your girlfriends for impromptu dinners, movies, shopping outings, and the like whenever you feel like it? A group doesn't replace these other very important experiences with your friends, but the reasons for forming or joining a group are many. As we already touched on, belonging to a group lends legitimacy to a gathering in a woman's hectic life. It can offer a sanctuary for you to pursue an interest or passion within a community of talented, motivated, and like-minded women. A girls' group can help you to grow physically, mentally, and/or spiritually, in ways that far exceed a delightful afternoon spent looking for bargains with a couple of friends. We look forward to each meeting and come to rely on the group and its members.

For some of us, these groups can become family. As we move away from our own families, we seek out replacements for intimate, supportive relationships. And we seek out opportunities to gab. "Women need conversation and they need downtime," Kathy Patrick continues. "Time for yourself makes you appreciate everything else." And women's groups do become as reliable as relatives. It rained cats and dogs during Kathy's grand reopening at her bookstore/beauty salon, and she had a group of women from her book club helping the entire day—tricked out in umbrellas and wading boots. That kind of commitment is common among girl groups.

And I'm not using the word commitment lightly. Some of these groups have been in existence for decades and have lasted longer than many relationships. Carol Hamlin's Bible-study group was formed in the late seventies. Debra Lande's mah-jongg group has been in existence for at least twenty years (she's been in it for fourteen of them). The groups morph and change as members move away, but the remaining women are committed to the regular meetings.

These types of get-togethers aren't just fun and games; they are essential to many women. A women's group can feed the spirit, but it can also allow a woman to add and build skills that she can bring to other parts of her life. As Divas Uncorked member Callie Crossley says, "In a group, you can be creative outside your job and tap into all sorts of things you didn't do before. You can pursue a passion but also gain skills to bring to other parts of life. The Divas Uncorked have new kinds of empowering skills, which allow us to get more recognition at work."

The type of organization you choose to join or form depends on you and your passions. Do you desperately want to grow your portfolio? Do you want to learn a new craft? Do you just want a reason to connect with other motivated women? Sometimes world events will prompt you to act. When President George W. Bush made the decision to go to war, Jo Wharton's Cranes Fly for Peace organization (www.cranesflyforpeace.com) committed to making a thousand origami peace cranes and giving them away. To date, the organization has given away twelve hundred peace cranes around the world. What puts a fire in your belly?

And speaking of passion, what about men—wonderful, but ultimately uninivited, guys? Unless it's a man-bashing club, there's no reason to trash the less fair sex. Because girl groups are not about men! They are about women—supporting and encouraging women to grow and to feel they are part of a community. Using meeting time to focus on men is fine now and again—after all, they are part of our lives—but bringing men into the conversation too frequently can end up siphoning off the energy the group is trying to generate. And forget about inviting guys to meetings on a regular basis. "We did have a man show up one time," Jo Wharton says. "The group is promoted on the Internet as a 'women's circle,' and men want to come. What part of 'women' do you not understand? Women are so much more open and able to talk. With men and women together, hormones come out, and the group gets competitive." That said, it's a great idea to host a night, maybe a holiday party, where friends, family, and significant others are welcome. They might be curious and may enjoy a glimpse into this part of your life, a part that keeps you jazzed and sharp and, well, happy.

This is not to say that belonging to a women's group is without challenges. The more people who belong, the more opportunities for con-flict. There are responsibilities to running a group: membership, hosting, coordination, scheduling, promotion—the list can go on and on. *Girl Group*

Confidential will walk you through the basics of planning your group, selecting members, creating guidelines, hosting fun gatherings, troubleshooting those pesky dynamics, and growing your club so other women can experience the power of your group. There's a lot to do—much of it fun—so let's not waste any more time in getting the show on the road!

GIRL GROUP CONFIDENTIAL

CHAPTER 1

Getting Your Girl Game On

You selected this book — or someone who knows you figured you'd like it — so you're not only interested in starting your own girl group, you're motivated and like being prepared, just like a Girl Scout. Congratulations! You realize the importance of girl power and you want to surround yourself with women. However, unless you're one of the lucky few, it's not always going to be a warm and fuzzy experience.

You can picture your fantasy book club: a group of agreeable, lovely women sitting around a fireplace drinking wine and trading insights about the meaty novel they plowed through, before the night degenerates — um, I mean, *evolves* — into juicy girl talk.

Or your women's running group: a few dedicated, fit women who meet every morning at 7:00 A.M. sharp for an energizing run through a charming part of town before cooling off over a cup of coffee at your favorite café.

Dream on.

While women's clubs, groups, circles, and organizations have the potential to be inspirational, motivational, and just plain *fun*, they also have the potential to be problematic. Consider your closest female friends. Can you picture all of them in the same room? Chances are, when you pool all your pals from childhood, college, work, and your neighborhood, you have a group of gals with a variety of interests and personalities. They have one thing in common — you — and that doesn't always make for smooth sailing, since different parts of your personality probably emerge with different friends. While your girlfriends will put on their best faces initially, belonging to a group that gathers regularly can wear on anyone's nerves if they dislike or are occasionally irked by another member.

So choose wisely and plan carefully. Before you send out a mass e-mail inviting every woman you know to join up, stop! Step away from the computer and map out your goals (no matter how vague) and the structure (no matter how ridiculously detailed) of your female dream team. While it seems a simple thing to invite your best pals over for a weekly poker night, a bit of planning will go a long way toward ensuring everyone's a winner and no one is left feeling put out, ticked off, or underwhelmed.

WHAT'S THE PLAN?

Let the following exercises help you narrow your focus, clarify your goals, and cover issues you may not have thought of when you decided to start your own club.

I want to start a women's club to:
a. learn something new
b. socialize with female friends
c. get to know new women
d. indulge my hobby
e. advance myself professionally

Knowing why you want to start a club will help you determine how lighthearted or serious, structured or easygoing the club should be. Getting together over a shared passion is much different than getting together to shoot the breeze or to network for professional reasons. You need to ask yourself why you want to start a group—let alone one consisting entirely of women—in order to zero in on what you actually need from a group that you couldn't do on your own or with a close friend.

When I start something, I tend to:
a. take baby steps to stay within my comfort zone
b. do a lot of research before taking action
c. throw myself into it
d. start strong and then peter out

Having some self-awareness, particularly an understanding of your modus operandi regarding new and ongoing activities, will help you determine how dedicated you will be at the outset of your group venture and how you'll proceed once it's well under way. This is not to say you should scrap the idea if you know you tend to lose steam after your initial enthusiasm. But knowing that may tell you that you'll need to rely on the support and energy of other members to keep you and the group going.

I have:
a. one passion that I'm always interested in pursuing/at which I consider myself an expert
b. a few activities that I'm crazy about/obsessed with
c . many interests that I dabble in regularly
d. a tendency to get interested in something until I get bored with it or until a new activity captures my fancy.

If you are a jill-of-all-trades, master of none, a club might require more focus than you usually allot to one activity. On the other hand, it may keep your interest alive. The key if you are scattered in your interests is to spread responsibilities among several members so you aren't shouldering all the work yourself. Otherwise you'll become frustrated with the club and it will begin to seem like it's all work and no enjoyment.

I like to talk:
a. as little as possible
b. one-on-one
c. in small, intimate groups
d. in large, chatty circles

Figuring out your social comfort level is key to determining the number of women to include in your group. If you're a bit on the introverted side, invite just a few people to join at first. It would be unfortunate to start a group and then begin to feel alienated or shut down. If you love conversational chaos, invite a lot of women to join—and tell them all to bring a friend.

My schedule is:
a. wide open
b. full of pockets of free time
c. planned out weeks in advance
d. crazy busy

I think the group should meet:
a. weekly
b. every two weeks
c. monthly
d. whenever it's convenient for members

Being realistic about your schedule will allow you to figure out how frequently you should meet and whether you should plan meeting times in advance or just decide on each subsequent get-together at the end of each meeting. Of course, you may have a very different schedule than other members of the group, but if you're the one founding the club, you might want to set a meeting schedule that jibes with your lifestyle first and theirs second.

I think the group should:
a. always gather at my place;
b. share hosting duties;
c. meet outdoors;
d. meet in a rented or public space.

Do you have a lot of space? Do you love to have people over? Are you a bit of a control freak? If you answered yes to these questions, then you may be comfortable having the group meet regularly *chez vous*. However, if money or space is tight, consider rotating the hosting duties or meeting at another location altogether (a public park, quiet pub, or private dining room, for instance).

I like:
a. peaceful gatherings
b. lively conversations
c. heated debates
d. total ruckus

This is a point not to be taken lightly: don't ask a lot of women to join your group if you're going to have a raging headache from the divas' din after each meeting.

I live for:
a. spontaneity
b. the unexpected
c. organization (agendas, calendars, and lists—oh my!)
d. total control

Again, if you are laissez-faire, you can choose to be laid-back and loosey-goosey about the club's structure. If, however, you are a slave to your schedule and live for organization, then you probably need to set some ground rules and select members who are responsible and conscientious.

The word that *best* describes me is:
a. reliable
b. easygoing
c. social
d. earnest

Woman, know thyself. If you really think about your dominant personality traits, it will be easier to select other women for your group. If you're extremely reliable and organized, you might not want to ask your flaky friend to join. If you want to start a political activism organization, think carefully before inviting a hardcore party girl. Beyond those listed above, consider what other adjectives you'd use to describe yourself.

When it comes to money:
a. I find it hard to get friends to pay up
b. I need to be frugal—money's tight
c. I don't mind shelling out some bucks for the occasional good time
d. I don't really worry about money or whose turn it is to pay (it all evens out in the end)

It may seem obvious, but don't start a high-end wine or dinner club if you can't afford it. Instead, if you're interested in wine, start a wine club but stipulate that bottles shouldn't cost more than ten dollars. If you want to start a dinner club, have members take turns hosting a dinner party instead of going out to new hot spots. The Boston wine club Divas Uncorked recommends picking women with similar careers and economic situations to join your group. It creates a level playing field when it comes to travel, dues, and meetings.

These multiple-choice exercises are not intended to conjure up nasty flashbacks of the SAT. Rather, they are designed to get you in touch with yourself, your needs, and the kind of group you really, honestly want to form. If you have a crazy schedule, you should probably set up monthly meetings far in advance. Map out a whole year's worth of meetings so they get scheduled in everyone's planners and so that other obligations get worked around your gathering. If vying for attention in a large group drives you insane, resist the urge to invite every woman in your address book. Invite ten women—tops. You can always invite more women down the road, but after you've invited forty-seven of your closest friends you can't trim the group back without incurring hurt feelings.

Here are a few more particulars to mull over while you're in the planning stage (see Chapter 8 for more information on each type of group):

Kind of group:

_____   financial club (investment, budgeting, finance)

_____   book club

_____   culture club (movies, art, theater, music, TV)

_____   career club (networking, life coaching)

_____   gaming group (cards, bingo, board games, casino outings)

_____ craft circle (knitting, quilting, scrapbooking, beading and jewelry making, journaling, needlepoint, crochet, candle making)

_____ interest club (cooking, writing, wine tasting, travel, bird-watching)

_____ sporting club

_____ activist or emotional support group

_____ spiritual gathering (Bible study, meditation, Kabbalah, Wicca, Buddhism, divination)

_____ spa party

_____ other

Size of group:

_____ fewer than five

_____ five to ten

_____ ten to twenty

_____ more than twenty

Frequency of meeting:

_____ daily

_____ weekly

_____ every two weeks

_____ monthly

_____ every two months

Venue:

_____ your home

_____ different members' homes

_____ restaurant, bar, coffee shop

_____ outside

_____ other

Expenses:

_____ none, except any cost of hosting

_____ some, in the form of dues to cover general expenses

_____ quite a few, for travel, supplies, investing, extravagant hosting, and so on

Qualities that members should ideally possess:

_____ energy
_____ focus
_____ dedication
_____ vision
_____ imagination
_____ creativity
_____ patience
_____ organization
_____ warmth
_____ intelligence
_____ physicality
_____ optimism
_____ ability to stimulate/challenge others
_____ ability to listen/be quiet
_____ peacefulness
_____ thoughtfulness
_____ supportiveness
_____ loquaciousness/chattiness

CHARTS ARE YOUR FRIEND

OK, it sounds ridiculous, but creating charts of different groups of friends can help illustrate the likelihood of member compatibility. If you have several very distinct circles of friends—college buddies, coworkers, neighbors, and so on—a Venn diagram may prove useful. A Venn diagram represents sets (or groups of friends) as circles, with the sets' relationships to one another expressed through their overlapping positions, so that all possible relationships between the sets are shown.

To make your Venn diagram, draw a circle for each group of friends. Each circle should overlap the others slightly so that there is a space in the middle of the Venn diagram representing a segment of your friends that would get along with one another. Make sense?

For example, let's say Jen, Jane, and Jill are your coworkers; Lisa, Lynn, and Laura are your neighbors; and Martha, Meg, and Maxine are your college pals. Draw three circles (representing your three groups of

Charting the Right Mix

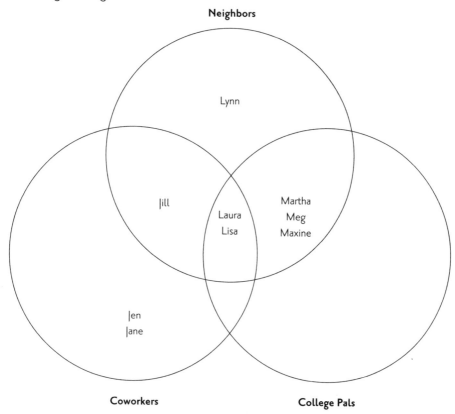

Neighbors

Lynn

Jill

Laura
Lisa

Martha
Meg
Maxine

Jen
Jane

Coworkers

College Pals

friends). Label one circle "coworkers," one "neighbors," and one "college pals." Now think about each person. Jen is often uptight and bossy; Jane is much younger than most of your friends and often makes hasty decisions and inappropriate comments; Jill, however, is reasonable and mature with a good sense of humor. You think Jill might mesh with your other friends, especially since she met your neighbor Laura at a pub one night and they got on like a house on fire. Laura is very chatty but doesn't take offense when you tell her to can it; Lisa is a committed soccer mom who is great at making snacks and being a caregiver; Lynn is rather nosy and seems very needy and desperately in want of a friend. And as far as your college pals go, they all rock, in your opinion. Why else would you still be friends with them a decade after you graduated? True, Martha is really busy with a high-powered career, Meg can't hold her liquor, and Maxine has a touch of ADD, but they are all terrific, true friends.

What next? Put Jill, Laura, Lisa, Martha, Meg, and Maxine in the shared part of the diagram's circles. With you, that's a group of seven. (As long as it's not a wine or spirits club, Meg should be fine with an occasional glass of wine during a meeting, right?) You've got the core of your group. And these women, if they are interested in joining, might have a few friends who also fit the club bill. Of course, they'd have to be interested in the theme of your group, but at least you have a mix of women who, based on careful thought and mathematical charting, you suspect would mesh well.

Flowcharts

You can also try creating a flowchart for each member to test suitability.

Make up a chart based on your critical criteria for membership. For instance, if you want to start a hiking club, must-have qualities for members might include fitness, a love of the outdoors, and reliability.

To wit:

POTENTIAL MEMBER

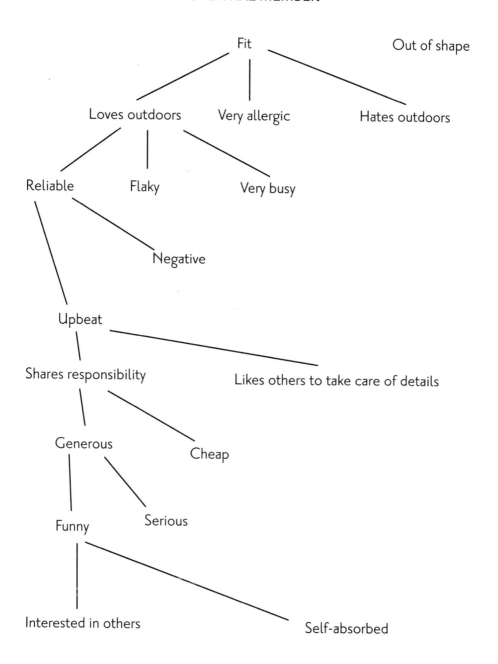

As you can see, all qualities in the flowchart are not considered equal. Obviously, it's more important that a woman be fit and upbeat in a hiking club, than serious and self-absorbed, but if she's unable to laugh when you get lost in the woods or talks incessantly about her boyfriend during a two-hour hike, she might not be the most welcome companion during your outing.

BUDGETS

Money is a sticky issue in most relationships. In fact, many a friendship has ended because one friend consistently scammed out on the bill or regularly "forgot" to bring cash along and the other friend was unable to confront her about it. When it comes to your organization's finances, forecast every expense as best you can, and do it in writing. The more detailed you are, the less likely that any member will be surprised or upset about the expense of the club, and the less likely that any member will get away with not contributing.

Budgeting will also help to determine whether members will have to pay dues and, if so, how much.

Here are a few things to budget for:
- beverages
- food
- room rentals
- postage
- printing, photocopying
- office supplies: folders, printer paper/ink, business cards, name tags, and so on
- books (for research)
- tech support and hosting: Web design, Web site host, ISP services
- domain name registration
- accounting software or ledgers
- phone bills (if long-distance calls are frequent and necessary)
- transportation (for rental cars or gas expenses on outings)
- scholarship fund
- volunteer or outreach programs
- T-shirts, hats, or other club memorabilia

GIVING YOURSELF A NAME

Brand yourself. Go ahead, it's OK. Not only is it fun and will give your group an added sense of togetherness from the get-go, it will lend your group a legitimacy that members and outsiders will respond to. And it will make it easier when you want to get T-shirts made or incorporate yourself.

Jot down a few possible names. What's the defining characteristic of the group? Do you want your city or state to be part of the title? The Nebraska Nitters would be great for a knitting circle, and the Writing Lifers would be a terrific name for a writing support group.

The Pulpwood Queens of East Texas, now a nationally franchised book club, is so named because pulpwood (quick-growing trees that are turned into paper) is a main industry in the area of Texas where the club was formed.

Carol Hamlin is one of the original members of a Lutheran Bible-study group started in the late seventies in St. Paul, Minnesota. She describes how the group originally selected a name: "Ladies' circles used to be the backbone of the Lutheran Church—cleaning church, making luncheons, caretaking the physical body of the church, performing good works. Each ladies' circle took the name of a woman in the Bible. So to honor the tradition of the ladies' circle, we also named ourselves after a woman in the Bible. However, as an act of defiance, we chose a renegade who was much maligned. Abigail wouldn't rise to the surface as the cream of the crop by men writing the Bible; therefore, we called ourselves Abigail's Circle."

Members of the Divas Who Dine, a high-powered lunch group in New York, Miami, and Las Vegas, came up with their name after chatting with real ladies who lunch, at their first lunch date. They thought it a playful take on "ladies who lunch."

Names have the potential to carry enormous power (conveyed to others and to the people who bear them), so choose yours carefully.

So now you know what kind of club you want to form, and you've compiled your wish list of members. You even know what you'd like to call your group. It's time to get crackin' and get your group together. Good times are a-wastin'!

JOINING AN EXISTING GROUP

Why go to all the trouble of putting your own group together when the perfect one already exists? Or does the prospect of forming your own group seem overwhelming, even for someone as motivated as you?

If you know of a group you want to join, look on the Internet for the group's Web site or even a contact number, or simply ask around for a contact name.

If you don't know of a group but are interested in joining an existing one, there are a few things you can do. First, determine what kind of group you want to join. You may be interested in the social aspect of a women's group but don't exactly know which one would float your boat. If you're crafty, you might consider a knitting circle. If you are a career gal in search of like-minded power women, look for an investment, networking, or industry organization. If you don't have a jones for any club in particular, think about joining an outdoors or hiking group to meet new people and participate in a fun activity at the same time. Food or wine clubs will definitely provide a social outlet, if that's the main consideration. The questions in this chapter that help you focus on your reasons for forming a club can also be used to determine what kind of club to join.

Once you've figured out what kind of group you want to hone in on, you need to track one down. Again, your trusty search engine can help you scour the Web for a local group that fits the bill. Try a few combinations of key words (such as "women," "knitting," and Tucscon, or "knitting," "circle," and "Arizona") and look at local city guides. Call a business that's related to your interest, such as a bike shop for a cycling group or an independent bookstore for a book club, and ask the manager or owner if she knows of a group. Put the word out with your friends so they can be on the lookout for an appropriate group for you.

Contact the group and express your interest. Ask if you can attend a meeting to get a sense of the group and its members. Unless it's got some top-secret activities going on, chances are this will be agreeable and you can get a firsthand view of the group's mission and the personality dynamics. Ask questions about the history of the group, its agenda, financial obligations, and its expectations of you should you become a member. Be courteous and enthusiastic about the group (follow up with a thank you card); even if you decide not to join—chances are you'll run into one or more members again. One woman could become a friend, another a business contact. Leave the channels of communication open and full of good will.

CHAPTER 2

Assembling the Group

Group dynamics are a curious thing. While you may get along swimmingly with your friends during solo or small get-togethers, bringing all of your favorite women together can be a recipe for disaster. So think carefully before extending invitations. Avoid a tense gathering by thinking about your friends' strengths, weaknesses, propensity for dominating a conversation or sulking for hours on end, reliability, and basic kindness. What unique qualities or skills can they contribute to the group? Assess their individual personalities, not to mention your relationship with each of them. While we'll get to what to do when there's dissension in your ranks, it's best to avoid starting out with a contentious group.

You may have reasons for keeping the group small; if so, member selection is critical. Debra Lande's San Francisco mah-jongg group consists of five members: four play, and the fifth acts as an alternate should someone miss the gathering; she gets to kibitz and make drink runs when she's not needed for play. "I had to be vetted before I went. They took me to lunch to check me out before I became the fifth member," Debra says. "For a long time, we had the same people. Roz was invited by Gail. Toby and Gail went to high school together in New York and have known each other for thirty years. We stayed steady for eight years or so and then Robin, the youngest woman in the group, left to become a rabbi. After cycling through a member, we now have someone who's been with us for two years."

Even if your group requires a limited membership, member selection can cause trouble. Think about how your friends might react if you *don't* invite them and what the ramifications might be. It pays to come up with some kind reasons why someone wasn't invited, in case you are called on the carpet about it. Try these out: "You are always so strapped for time and we really need people who can contribute a lot of time and effort." "Your career doesn't quite fit with the organization's mission statement." "There is only so much room in my kitchen, so I only picked the biggest foodies I know for the gourmet club." Sometimes there's no way to hide the fact that someone was pointedly not invited; in this case, it's best to be kind without giving too much explanation: "I'm sorry you're upset/feel left out, but this is the group of women I think will work best for this club." Having a few of these responses at the ready will help you avoid being blindsided by someone's hurt or anger.

Picking the right mix of women is key to your club's success. To this end, use the questions on the following page to help you assess your friends' individual personalities. (Don't worry, these insightful forms are not laborious—in fact, beyond helping you organize your club, they'll help you understand your friendship with each woman.) When you're done, you can assess the makeup of your proposed group and the likelihood that everyone will mesh well. Before assigning qualities to different women, however, use the same form to fill out a personality assessment of your ideal member (but be aware she doesn't exist). This way, you'll have an image in mind of who you'd like to see in the club, and a basis for comparing and contrasting potential members.

As you look ask yourself, how does each woman mesh with the traits you're seeking in a group member? Be cautious when assessing the qualities. While you may want a group that generates lively conversation, you don't want one entirely composed of chatty extroverts. Who's going to be listening to what they have to say? You should strive for a mix in personalities, but look for responsible people across the board.

Divas Uncorked founder and president Stephanie Browne was interested in wine, so she asked five friends to join a wine club and to select another person to join the group, resulting in a group of twelve members (she too asked one other woman). Twelve months, twelve meetings, twelve members to take turns hosting a dinner party. Voila! Other women have wanted to join the group, but the Divas made a conscious choice to keep the group small. A larger group would be too raucous and expensive for a monthly dinner party.

Sometimes the group just evolves organically from a church or other institution. Jo Wharton's women's circle, which looks at the goddess archetype and women's spirituality, developed out of a group that met in a

POTENTIAL-MEMBER PERSONALITY ASSESSMENT
Name:

Is she:
❑ a stickler for punctuality and detail?
❑ laid-back and frequently tardy?

Does she:
❑ tend to be a loner?
❑ stick to a few close pals?
❑ have a lot of friends?

Does she:
❑ prefer to stay home?
❑ live for going out?

Would you describe her as more of a:
❑ talker?
❑ listener?

If you told her something top secret, would she:
❑ lock the secret in her vault?
❑ spill the beans to the world as fast as she could?

Is she:
❑ financially solvent?
❑ always broke?

Is she:
❑ a great cook?
❑ hapless in the kitchen?
❑ possessed of a hearty appetite?
❑ always on a rigid diet?

Is her home:
❑ a dump?
❑ a showplace?
❑ comfortable and inviting?
❑ sterile and cold?
❑ spacious?
❑ tiny?

In your experience, is she a:
❑ fabulous hostess?
❑ disaster when entertaining?
❑ bit afraid to have people over?

What are her best qualities? Here are a few to get you started:
❑ dependable
❑ free-spirited
❑ fun
❑ gregarious
❑ optimistic
❑ thoughtful
❑ provocative
❑ impulsive
❑ organized
❑ industrious
❑ creative
❑ intelligent

Unitarian church. Carol Hamlin's Bible-study group is comprised of "raving liberal democrats, down to the last person. If a woman wasn't like-minded, I think it would be uncomfortable enough that she wouldn't come back." As you can imagine, the congregation of her Lutheran church leans to the left to begin with.

There are other similarities, aside from religious and political beliefs, to consider seeking out in members. While a member's hostessing skills, home, and financial situation might seem to be shallow concerns to consider, let's be honest here. If you are forming a movie club, and members will take turns hosting the group, you want to make sure each woman has the means to pull it off—not to mention a good-sized television! If you are putting together an investment club, you don't want members who won't be able to contribute or pull their own weight. Avoid any awkwardness by selecting those women who can share the responsibilities.

THE IDEAL MIX

If you are putting this club together with a friend or two, sit down and hash out an invite list. Now is not the time to be polite. Speak up if you have any reservations, no matter how vague, about a woman. Your instinct is a powerful tool, and it might be telling you that a particular woman could be problematic down the road or not mesh well with the rest of the group.

Perhaps you really like a woman but don't know her very well. Ask someone who knows her better to vouch for her character or attest to her personality. If that's not an option, spend some one-on-one time with her before considering inviting her into the club.

Some groups are no-brainers. If that's the case, God bless. Artist e Bond started Art Night with some former classmates from Philadelphia's Moore College of Art and Design and the University of the Arts. "We'd been out of school and stopped making art because we were working," she explains. "We were getting sad and anxious. So we got together at one woman's house on Monday nights (weekly at first), and we'd bring whatever it was we wanted to work on. We had a show at Moore and started to give ourselves projects. Each month, we'd give ourselves a word (such as "journey") and make art around that. After three or four years, everyone started getting busy, so it dropped to once a month, and then we'd meet on birthdays."

Groups can come together easily and organically, but you will still benefit from careful thought about your club's makeup at the outset, even if it's only to consider everyone's personalities, strengths, and weaknesses.

SIZE MATTERS

Along with the ideal personality mix are issues of size. As you'll find throughout this book, all sizes of groups are discussed. A passel of women works for some organizations but for others, it's just too unwieldy or unpleasant to deal with. While nearly all of the advice can apply to any size group (setting up a Web site or dealing with a troublesome member, for example), some of the information (booking meeting spaces, franchising your group) may not apply… at least not now. But this book will serve as a reference down the road when you and your group may find itself ready to spread its wings. So if you don't think some of the sections apply to you, skim over them for a general understanding of the various issues that may confront you later on, and focus on the salient portions now.

EXTENDING AN INVITATION

If you're ready to invite select women to join your group, why not consider an alternative to a quick phone call or e-mail? While those methods of communication are appropriate for an informal gathering, you can convey that you want to take your group seriously from the get-go. If you extend a thoughtful, formal invitation, the prospective members will be more likely to respond with the same level of consideration.

Handwritten Invitation: Buy formal invitations at a stationer and fill out the "five w's": who, what, why, where, when. Ask each woman to RSVP; leave the details to be revealed at your first gathering. The mystique and old-world charm of a thick, white invitation will pique each gal's interest to the point that she won't be able to stay away!

Press Kit: Treat your invitation like a press packet. Send women a folder jammed with information about the club, along with a letter inviting them to join, information sheets about other members, potential activities, supply lists, the first meeting time and location (with a map, if necessary); include something fun—such as a novel you'd like to kick off your book club with (*The Jane Austen Book Club,* perhaps?) or a map of a nearby national park for your outdoors club. It doesn't have to be expensive, but a dash of creativity and a professional presentation are sure to get everyone jazzed from the get-go.

Evite: The benefits to using an electronic-invitation Web site such as Evite (www.evite.com) are many: the site keeps everything organized; information remains housed in one spot that prospective members can return to again and again; reminders are sent out automatically; and everyone can see who's been invited and who's responded. You can also choose from a wide variety of graphics to customize an attractive e-mail. For ease of use and organization, it's hard to beat Evite.

E-mail: You can certainly extend an invitation by e-mail—it is the communication medium of choice these days—but treat it like real correspondence. Resist the urge to forgo capitalization and punctuation and litter the message with emoticons. Instead, write a draft and spend some time rereading and editing it to make sure you are conveying the right tone and including all the pertinent details. If it's an option, choose a fun font and consider using a background color or colored text. Just make sure it's legible.

Phone Call: While it may seem that calling your friends is the quickest method of invitation, you will most likely spend considerable time chatting with each woman about the club and other topics. A ten-minute call can easily turn into an hour-long one with a good friend. If you do choose to invite people by phone, keep a cheat sheet with notes in front of you and check off each detail as you communicate it to each member. This will ensure that everyone is getting complete and consistent information.

No matter which method you choose for your invitation, be as detailed as possible. Indicate the location and frequency of meetings, the size of the group, any dues and responsibilities, your contact information, and the date by which you'd like a response. If you choose to tease prospective members with a formal invitation and the promise of more specific information at the first meeting, make sure to have handouts or folders that detail all the specifics of the club available for everyone when they arrive.

A Backup Plan for When Someone Declines

Assembling your group will initially feel like a sorority rush or the NFL draft. A few of the friends to whom you give "bids" will decline to join, at which point you might ask women from your backup pool to join. The tricky thing will be making them feel as if they are first-round selections. So don't wait too long before inviting the second round. If you are giving a gal short notice before the first meeting, apologize and say you are a bit behind because you've been crazy busy. If she realizes she's second string, tell her that you initially wanted to keep the group very small but soon realized that more members like herself would enliven the group immeasurably. When all else fails, flatter!

What Happens When One Member Objects to Another?

You invite a collection of women you think will get along. But something unexpected happens when you mention one woman's name to another friend you've invited. She flips out! How were you supposed to know that they have bad blood that goes way back? Or that your friend just doesn't like or trust the woman and that nothing will change that?

Well, there's no use wringing your hands and playing the "what if" game—as in "What if I had done more research about everyone's relationships?" or "What if I had asked a couple of my close friends for advice in putting the group together?" The only thing to do is move forward. You have two basic choices: disinvite one of the women, or tell your friend with the issue to suck it up or stay away. The latter is the less sticky approach. It puts the burden and the decision back on your friend. She will have to decide whether to give the other woman a chance, suffer her silently, or avoid her and the group altogether. Chances are she'll be more interested in being in the group than in holding on to her dislike. At least let's hope so.

But that wasn't the case for a new chapter of Divas Who Dine. A key point person couldn't stand a woman who was invited at the last minute (as a referral from another city's chapter). Founder and president Zoe Alexander remained neutral and told her point person that she wasn't going to disinvite the potential member. "We're all adults here. I've been in plenty of rooms with people I don't like," Zoe says. "If you don't get along with someone, you have to be woman enough to show up and be professional. It is important for me not to give in to a request like this even once, because then there'd be a precedent." The disgruntled woman ultimately didn't show up—only hurting herself in the long run. But perhaps it was better for the group, since it sounds like she holds a mean grudge.

Keeping Numbers In Check

Make sure you let all the women know that you want to control the group size and that they shouldn't feel free to invite whomever they want. Tell them that you put a lot of thought into each invitee—at least initially. Give it six months or so before considering new members. By that time, the group will have jelled, members will have bonded, and you'll be ready to throw some new energy and personalities into the mix. However, at that point you might want to be even more selective with new members. See Chapter 7: Growing Pains & Gains, for more information on the application process.

WHEN GEOGRAPHY GETS IN THE WAY

Just because your friends live in far-flung locales doesn't mean that you can't meet with any frequency. Liesa Goins, a magazine editor in New York, meets with her childhood friends regularly, despite the fact that they live all over the country. The women created a group on Yahoo! so they could stay in touch regularly. When one woman sends an e-mail to the group address, everyone receives the message. The Yahoo! account also includes a database with the members' contact and family information.

But that's not all they did—the group set up a monthly conference call through a 1-800 service. Here's how it works: for the price of one long-distance phone call, everyone calls into one number at the same time, punches a code, and gets plugged into a conference call. And lest you think this is a casual group of girlfriends, the five members started a scholarship fund in memory of a friend who died of leukemia. They were nineteen years old when they set up the fund, and more than a decade later the fund is going strong. During their monthly calls, the women read scholarship applications and discuss candidates and fund-related business.

Artist e Bond's group keeps in touch with its members who move or travel through a "moving journal." She got the idea from Art Night members Dee and Barb. "You keep a journal for a couple of months and then send it to another woman to write in," e says. "Dee's group has volumes and volumes of them, which have taken them through breast cancer, kids, all sorts of life events. So when my friend Sherri went to Italy for a year, I bought her a box with seven journals, and we sent them back and forth. She got used to writing to me and it became a recording of her experience, as well as a way to connect with me."

So whether you have a group of high school or college friends you'd like to talk with regularly, or you have a group that's been chugging along despite one member's moving away, there are ways to keep in touch and to keep your conversations fresh and relevant. Physical distance doesn't have to translate into distance in your relationships!

CHAPTER 3

The Rule Book

As a rule, rules kind of stink. We look for ways around them. We often break them. But to live harmoniously and maintain some order in the world and in your club, they are sometimes necessary.

Maybe you want your group to have a very laid-back environment without a lot of structure. If that's the case, you might just want to get your pals together for dinner once in a while. Even if the vibe is mellow, setting up a few ground rules will help eliminate confusion and irresponsibility down the road. Think about it: putting together a rule book or handbook at the outset can provide some guidelines for when members act out. It is a great thing to be able to reference a page in your club's handbook when someone doesn't pay her dues in a timely fashion.

There's probably more to organizing your group than you think. For example, let's say you want to start a gin rummy club. It's not simply a matter of sending out an e-mail and gathering every few weeks. There's coordinating different members' schedules, serving up snacks and beverages, determining whether you'll meet at your place or you'll rotate hosting duties—not to mention deciding on rummy rules, on whether and how much to bet, and on whether the winnings will go into a big pot for future games or they'll go to a member each time. And let's not forget member etiquette: are there any ramifications for members who are always late or who frequently skip the gaming night? Maybe not, but even agreeing that it's not a big deal should be something that's spelled out from the get-go. Not quite as simple as it appeared on the surface, is it?

So take a bit of time, as painful as it may be, to knock out a few guidelines for your group. They don't have to be perfect or all-inclusive. You can always tweak as you go—new issues are bound to crop up as you settle into a groove. To help you get started, check out the main issues below and jot down a few notes about your ideal group structure.

THE NITTY-GRITTY

OK. Let's cover the basic points you'll want to address—whether in a sheet, pamphlet, or hefty book of rules—along with a few suggestions for guidelines your club might want to adopt.

Scheduling

If you can, schedule several meetings in advance, or just set a standing date, such as the first Tuesday of each month or every Thursday from 6:00 to 9:00 P.M. Women's schedules get filled up mighty fast these days, and it's best to have members work around meetings rather than trying to find a meeting that works for everyone a few weeks out.

For most groups, a monthly meeting is ideal. Donna Howard's Knock Three Times dinner/support group only meets every month or two. "We've found that if you meet too often, you start focusing on therapy issues and it got too deep, rather than just relaxing and enjoying each other's company," Donna explains. Maria Young's neighborhood book club meets the third Monday of the month. Members take turns hosting, and the hostess selects that month's book. Mocha Moms L.A. has monthly potlucks. "We keep time to catch up. After we take care of business, we're sitting around in our sweats and just say, 'What's going on?'" notes president Sherry Petrie.

Carol Hamlin's Bible-study group meets on the second Monday evening of the month. Planning is a bit trickier. "We meet in private homes, and the hostess provides the food. We tried to sign out meetings way in advance but that didn't work, so we do it during the previous meeting," Carol says.

Jo Wharton's weekly women's circle has the same issue. "We put out a schedule two months at a time. That's as far out that people want to commit to hosting in their house," Jo says. "We schedule three months in advance," says Debra Lande of her mah-jongg group. "We rotate at people's houses and we have an order: Gail, Roz, Toby, Debra, Jennifer. We meet every other week, sometimes every three weeks if people are out of town." Scheduling out a few months in advance is efficient. You don't have to drag your planners out at every meeting and negotiate times (and there's always a member who forgets her datebook). You can do it every few meetings instead.

Punctuality and Attendance

In order to have a successful, thriving club, it's critical that members show up. Duh, right? Life is sure to get in the way from time to time, but treating attendance and punctuality seriously from the beginning will set the tone necessary to keep members respectful of the club and one another. Agree that all members should do their best to work other errands and appointments around meetings. Schedule meetings several months in advance and hold them at the same time to minimize member conflicts. You can also set up automatic e-mail reminders to go out a week or two in advance of the gatherings.

Require members to call the club president or another member twenty-four hours in advance if they have to miss a meeting. (This holds for the president as well, who should alert another member.)

You could give every member one "pass" during the year where they can miss a meeting, no questions asked. Missing more than one is unacceptable and should require an explanation to the entire group.

Expect attrition. There will be the members who stick and those whose attention is focused elsewhere. "There used to be seventy women in my church's moms' group, now [there are] only nine. Once kids hit a certain age, the mothers' group [isn't] as much of a priority," says Maria Young of her Grand Rapids group. And sometimes attrition is temporary and seasonal, as life butts in. "Our attendance is very regular, which might have a lot to do with the fact that women are retired," says Carol Hamlin of her St. Paul group. "January to March is a problem, however, because snowbirds head south, and our attendance might dip to six members."

Respect

Don't think that the rules stop once you are gathered together. While most women are well versed in the basic tenets of civility, it pays to spell a few out in advance so no one ends up feeling scolded, called out, or embarrassed down the road.

For instance, ask that members raise their hands during a discussion to avoid interrupting one another. You can pass a marker around: whoever has it has the floor.

When members disagree—which they will, and often—demand kindness. If you sense a conversation spiraling out of control, use a predetermined code word to stop everyone in their tracks, and remind them to take deep breaths.

Implementing a rule or two will only foster and cement mutual respect among members.

Pulling Equal Weight

Depending on the nature of your club, you may need to assign a variety of tasks to members. Obviously, for a book or film club, this isn't necessary. But even in the most laid-back of groups, each member should take her turn hosting, selecting the topic of the next meeting, preparing notes or questions, and making or bringing refreshments. Don't leave it to the most enthusiastic volunteers to do all the work. At some point, they won't be so enthusiastic!

And while you're putting together your rule book, consider adopting the following ground rules to ensure that everyone's on the same page:

- No men allowed.
- No male bashing allowed.
- No kids or pets allowed.
- No foul moods allowed.
- No cell phones allowed.
- No side conversations allowed while a meeting is in progress.
- Everyone should bring a snack or beverage.
- Members should come prepared (i.e., finish the book selection or any homework or action items that are due) or not come at all.
- Any griping or moaning must be kept to the first ten minutes.
- Dues are collected at the beginning of every meeing, or once a year by a set date.
- Decisions must be approved by a majority of members.

AGENDAS

Does your group require an agenda? If you have more than one piece of business to address during a meeting, then yes, it does. The agenda can be jotted down by the group leader to prompt her during the meeting, it can be sent out via e-mail in advance of the meeting, or it can be distributed to each member at the meeting so they can follow along.

The president or head of the club doesn't have to be responsible for the agenda. You can simply divide things into "old business" and "new business." Designate a member to maintain the agenda. Ask that members e-mail her any items for the agenda a day or two prior to the meeting. That should give the point person time to organize, prioritize, and print or send out agendas. During a meeting, the point person should cross out items as they are dealt with, or note which items need to stay on the agenda (as "old business" for future meetings). Taking a few notes will also go a long way toward keeping everyone accountable from meeting to meeting.

If a discussion has gone on for some time, it can be tempting to just move on to a new subject without resolving anything. Agree that at the end of each point of business, the person leading the discussion will sum up the conversation, any decisions that were made, and note any action items that need to be addressed at the next meeting or down the road. Assign a member to each action item to move the task along and to keep someone accountable. Jot down these action items and their assigned members. They've just become future agenda items!

Be aware that, inevitably, poor time management will creep in. The first items always suck more time from the meeting than you anticipate — since, after all, you've got the whole rest of the meeting to get to the remaining agenda items, right? Well, not when after two items you've already spent an hour of the two allotted. Ask members to include how much time they need when they submit agenda items. Put that time down next to each item, and keep an eye on the clock. If a member runs low on time, gently interrupt and ask if she can sum up the conversation and identify action items for the next meeting. If you are consistent with this approach, no one will take offense at being cut off. You can also table the conversation until the end of the meeting when, if there's time, you can return to the subject if it merits it.

Sample Agenda

June 18, 2006
The Seattle Sailing Sisters

Old Business
Dues report (Diane; 10 minutes)
Calendar of events; see attached schedule (Pam; 10 minutes)

New Business
Disadvantaged-youth sailing clinic (Lisa; 30 minutes)
Women's Expo participation (Jane; 15 minutes)
Independence Day sailing party (Pam; 15 minutes)

Open Forum
(for items that didn't make the agenda, or general conversation)

DELEGATION

That brings us to division of labor. If you're planning to take care of all the details of your club, why start a club at all? Part of belonging to a group is reveling in teamwork and leaning on one another. Even if you're Wonder Woman, there's bound to be a task to which someone else would be better suited. You can't be good at absolutely everything, especially if you're trying to do it all. Instead, try assigning things based on skill sets or willingness or, if you're lucky, both.

Philadelphia's Art Night group plays to people's strengths. "Two people are good at hanging work; I hate to hang work, but I'm good at anal details; Sherry's really good at writing and public relations, so those tasks don't seem like work to her," artist e Bond explains. "There are nights when everyone comes together to help. Some can't cut a straight line with an X-Acto knife, so they punch holes or glue instead. And for the members who aren't good at any art stuff, well, they help out with the food or cleanup."

If you know a member isn't particularly responsible but she volunteers to manage the club checking account, try to redirect her to a less-important task like researching guest speakers (speak to her strength of dealing with people) or pair her up with one or two other members to share the duties. Here are some areas of responsibility you might want to delegate:

- agendas: setting, creating, running
- minutes: taking and distributing meeting notes
- leading meetings or discussions
- hosting
- membership
- finances
- promotion
- guest speakers: booking, coordinating, handling
- field trips
- ads and sponsors
- Web site responsibilities
- community relations
- community service, philanthropy
- fund-raisers

Take a tip from Jennifer Ashare, a member of New York's Divas Who Dine, and special events director for B.R. Guest. "Use who you know. Don't be afraid to ask the group for help. While the leader wants to show that they are doing it themselves and getting it done, the newbie in the corner might know someone. Asking around gives more people ownership in the group, and they feel invested in wanting to make it work," she suggests.

Elections

If your group is large, you might want to consider holding democratic elections. Take nominations for top positions at one meeting and hold elections at the next. You can either choose to have one member nominate another and have someone second the nomination, or you can simply have members nominate themselves. Sometimes there will only be one willing candidate, but when more than one member wants a post, it's best to vote anonymously rather than by hand raising or the like.

Keep the time short between nominations and elections; you don't want members' energies focused on campaigning when there's club work to be done. Anyone running for office should have enough history with the group that members have a sense of the candidate's personality, trustworthiness, and ability to stick to something. If you like, you could have each candidate give a short speech before the election to state her plans should she be elected to a position.

For the election, distribute a ballot to each member at the meeting, and collect them after a short time. Unless your membership is in the hundreds, you can probably count the ballots during the meeting and announce the winner before the end of the evening (make sure you have two women counting and checking so there are no complaints about the process).

Positions you might want to elect include president, vice president, treasurer, secretary, and various chairs, such as membership chair. Too many titles, however, means not enough members to help the elected officials, so be judicious when setting up official positions.

Who Decides?

Sooner or later, an issue will arise about which there will be differing opinions. It may be about how to raise funds for a charity or about whether the meetings' structure should change. In each case, a decision will have to be made. But before that decision can be reached, another decision must be resolved. Namely, who decides? There are pros and cons to reaching a group consensus on issues and to making executive decisions (i.e., the president or founder makes the call).

"We tried to do things democratically at first but it takes too much time. If you try to do everything by committee, you may never get anything done," says Zoe Alexander, founder of the Divas Who Dine. "In the beginning, there was some stepping on toes. Trying to work with someone on a project that was my baby was challenging, but my vision had to come through. If you don't make this clear up front, you could wind up displaying passive-aggressive behavior. But on the flip side, everyone's very vocal in the group and tells you what's working well and what can be worked on. One member, for instance, said the introductions people were giving about themselves at each meeting were way too long, so we implemented a sixty-second rule."

Not all issues are created equal, and some issues will need to be put across to the group or to a committee. Use your discretion. Choosing a color for your Web site is one thing, deciding to meet twice a month instead of once a month is another. Think about what will impact your members, and seek out their opinions on those matters. Don't worry about sweating them with the small stuff unless it becomes an issue for one or more members.

EVEN A RULE CAN BE COOL!

Rules and guidelines don't have to be boring and business-y all the time. Members of the Pulpwood Queens, the nationally franchised book club that originated in Jefferson, Texas, are required to wear tiaras at every meeting. And you've probably seen members of the Red Hat Society out and about sporting hats and clothing in shades of red and purple. Incorporating festive and fun elements will ensure that members look forward to each and every meeting.

Here are a few fun ideas to implement:

- Allot the first fifteen minutes strictly to catching up on celebrity gossip or one another.
- Feature a different cocktail (hostess's choice) at each meeting.
- Make a rule that anyone who interrupts another member has to put a quarter into a jar.
- Take a Polaroid or digital photo of the group at the start of each meeting to capture the moment.
- Begin each meeting with a prayer or blessing.
- Create a secret handshake or initiation ceremony. (Why should twelve-year-olds have all the fun?)
- Have the members buddy up, and assign different tasks to the teams throughout the year (a presentation on a group-related topic, a research project, soliciting a guest speaker, planning a trip, hosting a meeting, and so on).

Refer to other clubs or organizations for structure. Debra Lande's San Francisco mah-jongg club looks to the National Mah-jongg League (www.nationalmahjonggleague.org) for guidance. The organization publishes a newsletter and an annual card with the hands and rules for each year, and even sponsors cruises. Members of Debra's club pay the kitty the dollar value of each hand, as set forth by the NMJL. The money goes toward their annual retreat at a fabulous rental house north of San Francisco.

"We meet to play the game and to eat. We try not to talk during the game. Beforehand, during the meal, and afterward are the only talk times, which sometimes doesn't leave a lot of time to get caught up," Debra says. The group gets four or five hands in—plus dinner—before breaking up at 9:30 or 9:45. A little chatting, a lot of food, and even more mah-jongg. Pretty good structure, wouldn't you say?

As evidenced by various groups, lots of structure isn't always necessary. Sometimes you just want to get together for socializing, with a side of something interesting or educational. If you want to start an investment club, on the other hand, you need structure and commitment from all members.

Jo Wharton's Texas women's circle is very open. "People come and go, and some have been there from the beginning. A meeting could consist of eight or eighteen women," she says. The meetings themselves are equally open. "We may read a book and watch videos. We are always on the lookout for topical things to bring to the group; for instance, we watched *Iron Jawed Angels* [an HBO film about the suffragette movement] as well as a PBS documentary about a 1970s women's conference on the equal rights amendment. We recently had a woman do chanting and dancing, the theme was 'woman power.'"

MISSION POSSIBLE!

You've got your ideal group figured out. Super! But before you start extending invitations, let's think about your club and the point of it all. You don't have to pull a Jerry Maguire and write a mission statement and distribute it to prospective members in the dead of night. However, you should probably write down your goals for the group. If you want to foster camaraderie and friendship in your financial club, you should be clear with yourself and others about this at the start. Otherwise, you might have a couple of type A women who want to get down to business immediately and who think taking fifteen minutes out to chat and catch up with one another is a waste of valuable time.

In case you do want to write a mission statement, it might be helpful to know exactly what one is. Businesses that craft mission statements regard them as something between a slogan, or catchphrase, and an executive summary. Your mission statement should convey your group's story and goals in a concise manner. If the idea of a "mission statement" sounds too grand and formal for your little ol' running group or cooking club, call it something that you're more comfortable with, be it a credo, diva doctrine, synopsis, club crib sheet, bullet points, or rules to live by.

So how do you go about drafting your club statement? You can write one up yourself and submit it to your club for discussion. Or you could designate one of the first meetings for brainstorming with the group. Write everything down and then read it back to everyone. Whittle it down and come up with a rough draft before disbanding. E-mail or send the text to the group prior to the next meeting. Everyone can bring their comments to the next meeting and the statement can be finalized then.

The benefits of writing the first draft yourself are that you can write down your undiluted vision, you can probably do it quicker than the group would, and when you distribute it to the group for review you have a starting point. Anyone who has ever collaborated on a writing project knows that too many cooks in the kitchen can result in disagreement and delay. On the other hand, you do benefit from a wealth of viewpoints and ideas, and everyone appreciates feeling included and valued.

Regardless of how you choose to write your statement, there are several points to consider and questions to answer:

- Who is your group?
- What does your group do?
- What does your group stand for?
- Why do you want to have this group?
- Why is this group important to you, the members, and the community?

Don't worry about writing a missive. A good mission statement need only be a few sentences long. Just make sure it covers your group's most important points. Don't waste space talking about how awesome the group and the women in it are. The most important thing is that everyone in the group believes 100 percent in the message. It should accurately reflect the opinions and personalities in the group.

You don't have to start from scratch. Mission statements abound. Just a quick tour of some different club or company Web sites will provide a variety of creative mission statements for use as inspiration.

Here are a few mission statements from phony groups to inspire you:

"The Big Hair Book Club of Council Bluffs, Iowa, will dedicate itself to reading and discussing works of fiction, both classic and contemporary, on a monthly basis. In addition, we will dedicate ourselves to caring for our friendships with one another, during and outside of meetings."

"We, the members of the Miami Finance Foxes, pledge ourselves to analyzing and purchasing stocks from companies we believe to be ethical, female-friendly, innovative, and potentially lucrative. We will only purchase and sell stocks if 75 percent of the membership supports the decision. In addition, we will work to foster understanding of the stock market within the female community and support each other in issues of personal and professional finance."

The Red Hat Society, probably the best-known women's club out there, provides the following (real) statement on its Web site (www.redhatsociety.com, naturally):

The Red Hat Society Statement of Purpose:
"The Red Hat Society began as a result of a few women deciding to greet middle age with verve, humor, and élan. We believe silliness is the comedy relief of life, and since we are all in it together, we might as well join red-gloved hands and go for the gusto together. Underneath the frivolity, we share a bond of affection, forged by common life experiences and a genuine enthusiasm for wherever life takes us next."
—Sue EllenCooper, Queen Mother

The motto of the Pulpwood Queens book club is "where tiaras are mandatory and reading good books is the RULE! The sole mission of the Pulpwood Queens book clubs is to promote literacy and get America READING!" Pretty clear message, wouldn't you say?

New York City's Divas Who Dine lunch group defines itself this way:

"DWD is an exclusive, membership-only monthly networking luncheon group for young women who 'make things happen.'"

Sherry Petrie, president of Mocha Moms L.A., defines her group as "a support group for at-home mothers. We welcome anyone who believes in our mission statement: 'altering your lifestyle to be at home with children.'"

As evidenced by these declarations, a mission statement doesn't have to be long, but it *does* have to offer clarity and a raison d'être to your members and the public at large.

THE MONEY ISSUE

Even if your group is easy-peasy and the understanding is that each member will take a turn hosting, money issues will percolate beneath the surface. A member may feel that one hostess is cheap, only buying a bag of chips, a jar of salsa, and a two-liter bottle of soda when everyone else whips up numerous homemade dishes and breaks out several bottles of wine. No matter what, resentment will brew.

Unless, of course, ground rules about hostessing are agreed upon in advance. For instance, you could agree to a financial cap for refreshments, ors all contribute to a food-and-drink kitty each month so that a small fee would go to the hostess at each meeting.

Divas Uncorked started out with Ritz crackers and buffalo wings at meetings, and quickly ratcheted up to elaborate dinner parties with invitations, party favors, custom tabletop decorations, themes, complicated recipes, music, and of course, wine paired to the month's theme. One member, Barbara, built a French kiosk in her living room and an Eiffel Tower on the buffet table. Another member went with a Tuscan theme; while in Italy, she picked up small watercolor paintings to give as favors. Carolyn sent an invitation package in the mail: it was a little purse with travel stickers that functioned as a passport of sorts. For the dinner, Carolyn enlarged the stickers and made placemats out of them. Barbara and Karen both conducted blind tastings; Callie featured rosés for her In the Pink dinner. Two members highlighted South African wines at their meetings; one decorated her dinner table by pairing rustic African fabrics with crystal and silver. She served local cuisine with the South African wines and sent everyone home with crystal wine stoppers as favors.

Obviously, these events aren't inexpensive. To that end, each Diva gives twenty dollars to the month's hostess toward the wine. The group usually samples three or four different wines, meaning they need to have ten to twelve bottles on hand per party.

If you pay dues, create a refreshments budget and give each member a portion for hostessing fees. If you want to make sure everyone's using their monies for the meeting, ask that receipts be submitted. You certainly don't want a member to fall under suspicion for pocketing the money and putting out a sparse spread as a result.

Speaking of dues, it's important to craft a realistic budget and collect dues—being careful to collect them at a meeting and then follow up with anyone who "forgot" her checkbook, giving her a deadline. If she doesn't pony up by the date set, remove her from the group. Be firm about this. If a member knows you are serious, she will take her financial responsibilities seriously in kind. If you let her slack or give her one new deadline after another or you hem and haw over asking, she'll know she can get away with not paying on time—or not paying at all.

Set up a spreadsheet in an accounting program like Microsoft Excel with each member's name, dues paid (and owed), the date she paid them, the check number, and the date you deposited the check. You can easily highlight or bold the names of the members whose payments are outstanding.

Here's an example of a spreadsheet:

Member	Dues Owed	Date Paid	Check No.	Date Deposited
Adams, Marni	$75			
Worick, Jennifer	$75	9/10/06	3102	9/15/06

To increase club coffers, the group Mocha Moms L.A. holds fund-raisers—but those in charge are very careful to monitor funds. "We have a nice account set up. Under the national organization, we are allowed to have funds and to be compensated for what we do. But we voluntarily pay for Mocha Moms' dinners, and we took up donations to give a gift to a woman who miscarried. When the group pays for something, we ask members to fill out a form for check reimbursement and submit receipts. Both the treasurer and I sign off on it, and that's how we keep everything together. We give the member a check for [her] expenses," says president Sherry Petrie.

Your club might gather every two weeks to watch a film or every morning to jog. In these cases, it may not seem necessary to be bothered with finances. And you're right . . . for the most part. For normal meetings or gatherings, it might just make sense for members to pay for themselves or for a meeting's hostess to supply snacks and supplies. However, if you want to plan a retreat, trip, special event, or fund-raising project, set up a bank account. When you collect monies from members for a trip, for example, you can put them into an account and then issue one check for the travel or lodging.

Many banks offer checking accounts for low-activity businesses. With a minimum deposit of just one hundred dollars, you can open an account for your club and keep funds safe. Ask for details at a couple of your local banking institutions. To keep financial safeguards in place, decline an ATM card. Arrange for two or three members to have access to the account but distribute regular financial reports to the entire club. How do you choose who has access to the account? If the group's president doesn't change frequently, she's an obvious choice, as is the club founder or another longtime, trustworthy member. Elect or appoint a treasurer to handle funds. When new elections are held, remove the former president and/or treasurer from the account and add the new ones. As an additional precaution, you can require a countersignature on all withdrawals, meaning that two members have to sign a check or slip before a withdrawal can be made. Substantial funds or minimal monies will both benefit from a secure checking account with limited access but club-wide distribution of monthly or annual statements. And with a bank account, you can earn interest that can be put toward your holiday party or scholarship fund.

RULES OF CONDUCT

Obviously, the nature of your club and the various personalities of the women in it are going to dictate the flavor of your group, be it sassy, soulful, laid-back, or strict. The following points can be modified to stay in line with your group's character. Consider them when putting together your club's rule book especially if your group is big—or getting bigger.

- Guidelines for speaking/contributing to a conversation are always useful. For example, each month's hostess must come up with discussion questions (for a book club), or one member has to wait until another is finished before making a point. We are cut off in conversation by impatient individuals often enough; no need to do it to each other.
- No matter how strong the urge, members can't talk during movie screenings (gasping or silently weeping is fine, however). If someone does get chatty, she has to put money into a kitty or endure being pelted with popcorn.
- Tardiness results in some sort of public humiliation or ponying up a small fine.
- X number of absences results in a probationary period or exclusion from the club. Harsh, yes, but if everyone knows the rules up front, they can't argue the point.
- Raunchy language and anecdotes are always welcome. Belching and breaking wind are verboten.
- As in Las Vegas, what happens in the group stays in the group (including all discussions). You've got to foster trust. A breach of trust should bring a harsh penalty or tongue-lashing from one or all members of the club.
- If you have an outdoors activity, group leaders and driving duties should be rotated. If any members don't have a car or don't drive, ask them to pitch in for gas, or delegate them some other responsibility.
- Cell phones must be turned off during meetings. A polite reminder at the beginning of each meeting (at least initially) should drive home the rule.

Disciplinary Action

For minor infractions, consider the following actions/consequences:

- Require the member to dish out a small fine to the club kitty for refreshments or miscellaneous expenses.
- Deliver a gentle rebuke in private, by phone, or by e-mail.
- Throw non-messy food at her, such as popcorn or pretzels. Hey, it beats stoning!
- Delegate extra tasks to the offender, such as an ice cream run.
- Require her to wear a special hat or scarlet letter during the meeting.

- Have each woman tell the offending member how her actions made her feel.
- Force the transgressor to read aloud (with feeling) the lyrics of "Send in the Clowns."
- Request that she make a public apology to the group—again, with feeling.

For major infractions, consider the following actions/consequences:
- Ask the member to leave the group.
- Deliver a public or private tongue-lashing.
- Make her sit in the corner during a meeting.
- Suspend her from several meetings.
- Stage an intervention.
- Make the member cook dinner for the entire group.
- Require her to babysit for any member who asks, for a set period.

Of course, after reading through all the issues involved in setting up and running a girls' group, you may choose to abandon all formalities. "When we've tried to be more formal, that is, ask women to read something ahead of time, half the people come without having lifted a finger," says Carol Hamlin of her Bible-study group. "So we gave up over the years. Sure, it was annoying to some people, but it didn't become a flash point." Decide what is important to you and the other members, and decide what you can let go, and proceed from there. And again, adjust your rules and guidelines as the group evolves and outgrows the structure you put in place. Now that the hard stuff is out of the way, let's move on to an infinitely more "entertaining" activity: hosting!

CHAPTER 4

Hosting

The time has come. It's—gulp—your turn to host your club. You could put out chips and dip and pass around a pitcher of lemonade, but why take the boring route when you can zest up your group's meeting and become the hostess of whom legends are made and songs are sung?

But before getting your cheese plate together and popping in a Norah Jones CD, hold up. Take a few minutes to assess your group and its meeting needs. You'll be thankful that you did when you host a wildly successful meeting with great seating, proper lighting, delectable but easy snacks, and of course, sparkling conversation and energy.

First of all, let's look at a few specifics pertaining to your group.

KIND OF GROUP:

- ❏ financial club
- ❏ book club
- ❏ culture club
- ❏ career club
- ❏ gaming group
- ❏ craft circle
- ❏ interest club
- ❏ sporting club
- ❏ activist or emotional support group
- ❏ spiritual gathering
- ❏ spa party
- ❏ other

SIZE OF GROUP:

❑ fewer than five
❑ five to ten
❑ ten to twenty
❑ more than twenty

OK, let's stop there. While you may be keen on hosting your club, if it has grown to a size your home can't accommodate, be realistic. You might want to find another space for the meeting—outside or at a favorite pub, for instance. Members of the Divas Uncorked wine club in Boston take into account each Diva's home when scheduling their monthly wine dinners. One member doesn't have central air conditioning, so she hosts the group during the colder months. Another has an amazing outdoor deck, so she picks a summer month. Talk among yourselves about each member's home, and think creatively about how to take advantage of the various spaces.

For your part, think specifically about your home and your needs.

CONSIDER WHICH TWO OR THREE OF THE FOLLOWING PHRASES BEST DESCRIBE YOUR HOME:

❑ big and roomy
❑ small and cramped
❑ full of expensive furniture and objects
❑ minimalist
❑ messy
❑ scrubbed within an inch of its life

DECIDE WHICH ONE OF THE FOLLOWING PHRASES BEST DESCRIBES YOUR APPROACH TO ENTERTAINING:

❑ planning weeks in advance
❑ flying by the seat of your pants
❑ feeling anxious and fussy before, during, and after
❑ keeping things relaxed and laissez-faire

AND CHEW OVER THE FOLLOWING QUESTIONS:

- ❑ Do you have enough seating and space to comfortably accommodate your members and their activities (whether cooking, quilting, or watching a film with subtitles)?
- ❑ Is strong lighting or soft ambiance preferable for your activities?
- ❑ Do you have pets that need to be put somewhere during your gathering?
- ❑ Is anyone in the group allergic to your pets?
- ❑ Do you need to provide the group with any supplies or information?

YOUR SPACE

You may be taking it for granted that you're going to use your living room for your meeting. After all, it's the space where you hang out, and the couch is downright cushy. But with a bit of imagination and thinking outside the box (or living room, in this case), you may find that you have an even more suitable place to hold your meeting.

Do you have a great backyard or patio that could accommodate your group? If so, do you have plenty of chairs and appropriate lighting? How about a backup plan in case it rains?

Is your kitchen warm and roomy? If so, have your stitch 'n' bitch club congregate there. With some creative chair arranging, you'll be within arm's reach of snacks, so you won't have to keep running to refill the chip bowl.

If your group is small enough and your bed big enough, consider letting your movie club sack out on your bed as you watch the latest Almodóvar film. Shouldn't everyone be as comfy as possible?

Seating

You know to provide comfortable seating for all (and yes, large floor pillows can indeed provide a comfy place to plop), but there might be a member or two in the group who require more support, cushioning, or surface area. If you've ever noticed a woman bringing along her own chair pad or suffering in silence as she hung off a small stool, consider her when setting up the meeting space. And when the women arrive, don't call attention to your thoughtfulness, but do slip your arm through your special guest's and guide her to her seat, saying that you thought she might particularly enjoy the spot, that you picked this spot out just for her, or that you wanted to make sure she was seated next to you.

Lighting

I hate turning on an overhead light. I suspect a few of you feel the same way. Depending on your group, you might be able to keep from flipping the dreaded switch. Dinner groups or wine clubs call for atmospheric lighting; a movie club might prefer total darkness, to replicate the cinematic experience; a divination group might fancy candlelight to get in the proper spirit for a séance or tarot reading. However, if you have a club where it's important to read (book club—duh!—or investment group) or essential to see what you're doing (knitting circle or poker night), you might have to don a visor and deal with the brightness of overhead lighting.

If you feel your house isn't outfitted properly for your group's meeting, you can assess the space and make a few quick fixes. If you need strong lighting and lack overhead illumination, swap out your table- and floor-lamp bulbs for seventy-five-watt bulbs. Just make sure the shades can handle the wattage. If you don't have a lot of low or soft lighting for a mellow gathering, pick up a few inexpensive lamps at Target or Ikea, or better yet, create ambiance with a sprinkling of tea lights or groupings of pillar candles. Use Christmas lights throughout the year—stringing up small white lights always lends a festive touch. If the meeting will be held outside, place a few tiki torches around the space. If it's an option and the season is right, light a fire in the fireplace. Nothing creates a convivial feeling like a warm fire and good friends.

Decor

If you've got the tiki torches fired up or the fireplace blazing, consider taking everything a step further and creating a theme for your meeting. It doesn't have to be pricey, but with a bit of thought and energy you can create a memorable evening for your group, whatever its focus. Use the following ideas as a launching pad for your own imaginative meetings.

Indoor Themes

The Ladies Lodge: Think fireplace, think flannel, think fun! Place branches of pine or bowls of pinecones around the room, throw a few plaid flannel blankets over the backs of chairs and couches to bundle up in, and serve up mulled cider and comfort snacks (which is as easy as making grilled cheese sandwiches and cutting them into bite-size niblets). You can end the evening by toasting marshmallows in the fireplace and making s'mores. Send guests home with a pine-scented votive. Expect members to pledge undying loyalty to you and the group. The only danger in hosting such an evening is that you may be asked to take over hosting duties every month.

Zen Den: Create a tranquil space for your group by lighting candles, putting out plush pillows, and serving up green tea and healthy sushi rolls (which many supermarkets now make daily). Kick off the meeting with some gentle yoga stretches and deep breathing. This will help everyone release the stress of the day and focus on the topic at hand. Give members some lucky bamboo to take home so they can have a little touch of calm near them at all times.

Mardi Gras: For meetings that fall near Fat Tuesday, enliven the event with Mardi Gras beads or masks, some Cajun food, brightly colored fabrics draped over tables and chairs, and New Orleans jazz. To start the meeting, go around the group and ask them to describe their fantasy vacation or recount their wildest night.

Ladies Who Lunch: For Carol Hamlin's Bible-study summer retreat, she gave a nod to the past when coming up with a theme. "I went with a 'back to the fifties' theme," Carol says. "I purchased vintage luncheon sets that women in the Midwest would use for luncheons in the fifties and sixties. Dressed up in a housedress, gloves, and hat, they would go to each other's houses or farms, have a dainty luncheon, and chat. For my more informal retreat, members brought swimming suits, but I served food on luncheon plates and linen. I also served foods from the fifties, such as sandwich loaf [a bread loaf that features three different fillings—like egg salad, chicken salad, and watercress—and is frosted with cream cheese and adorned with vegetable flowers; see below for Carol's mother's recipe. It's too fabulous not to include!]. We sat around and chatted like you would at a traditional ladies' tea."

SANDWICH LOAF

This recipe comes from Carol Hamlin's mother, Helen Stueland, of Granite Falls, Minnesota. Feel free to substitute any filling you like for the three layers. And don't try to pick this up with your hands. You'll definitely need a fork to enjoy a slice of this Midwestern luncheon staple.

Ham-salad Filling

> 1½ cups ground cooked ham
> ¼ cup finely chopped sweet pickles
> ½ teaspoon prepared mustard
> ¼ cup mayonnaise

Combine and mix well. If too dry, add a small amount of cream or mayonnaise.

Parsley-butter Spread

> ¼ cup finely chopped parsley
> ¼ cup soft butter
> Dash of salt

Prepare parsley by stripping leaves from stems, placing leaves in small glass, and snipping with scissors until fine. Combine with butter and salt, and mix well.

Egg-salad Filling

> 5 hard-cooked eggs
> 2 tablespoons chopped pickle
> ¼ cup finely chopped celery
> ⅓ cup mayonnaise
> 1 teaspoon prepared mustard
> ½ teaspoon vinegar
> 1 teaspoon salt
> ⅛ teaspoon grated onion

Chop eggs very finely or put through sieve or ricer. Add remaining ingredients and mix well.

FILLING VARIATIONS (OR CHOOSE YOUR OWN):
Chicken-bacon Filling
Mix 8 slices of crisp, pan-broiled bacon, crumbled finely, with 1 cup finely chopped chicken, ¼ cup mayonnaise, 1 tablespoon finely chopped pimento, ¼ teaspoon salt, and ⅛ teaspoon pepper.

Shrimp-salad Filling
Mix 1 chopped hard-cooked egg, 1⅓ cups finely chopped shrimp, ¼ cup finely chopped celery, 2 tablespoons lemon juice, ¼ teaspoon salt, dash of pepper, and ¼ cup mayonnaise.

Cheese-pecan Filling
Mix one 3-ounce package of softened cream cheese, 1 cup finely chopped pecans (toasted), and ¾ cup well-drained pineapple.

Chopped Cucumber Spread
Mix ¾ cup finely chopped, peeled cucumber; ½ cup mayonnaise; ½ teaspoon salt and dash of pepper.

Other Ingredients:
    3 tomatoes, medium sized
    ¾ cup cucumber, peeled and finely chopped
    ½ cup mayonnaise
    ½ teaspoon salt
    Pepper, to taste
    8 ounces cream cheese, softened
    Parsley, nuts, radish roses, stuffed olives, edible flowers for garnish

ASSEMBLY INSTRUCTIONS:
Have all fillings prepared and butter softened for easy spreading. Cut crusts from large, unsliced loaf of bread (white or whole wheat), and cut in 4 uniform horizontal slices. (Note: This can be done at the bakery; they can cut it so that it doesn't tear. You can also get one loaf of white and one of whole wheat, and mix the layers for a more interesting and tasty version.)

Spread butter lightly on first slice of bread, then spread generously with ham filling. Spread second slice with butter and lay it, buttered side down, over ham filling. Spread top of that slice with a thin layer of parsley butter, then a layer of egg-salad filling, at the same thickness as as the ham filling. Spread third slice of bread with thin layer of parsley butter, and place this side over egg-salad layer. Spread top layer lightly with butter, and cover with overlapping thin slices of tomato. Combine and spread over tomatoes.

Top with fourth, unbuttered slice of bread. Press layers together firmly. Wrap tightly in moist cheesecloth or towel, and then waxed paper. Place on flat-surfaced pan or board, and chill at least 3 hours. Unwrap, place on serving platter with layers running vertically or horizontally as desired. Spread softened cream cheese over sides and top of loaf. Decorate as desired with parsley, nuts, radish roses, and/or stuffed olives. Use edible fresh flowers as additional garnish, if desired. Cut slices with an electric knife, and serve.

Serves 8–10

For a real "back to the fifties" luncheon, use glass luncheon plates that feature indentations for coffee cups; make a Jell-O fruit cocktail/mini-marshmallow salad topped with Reddi-wip; and finish off with "bars" (brownies, blondies, and so on) or slices of yellow, chocolate, or white cake with frosting. Carol cheated once and made a seven-layer lettuce salad rather than the Jell-O salad, which landed her in the seventies instead of the fifties.

Lady Luck Night: Remember, what happens in Vegas stays in Vegas, and so it goes for your meetings. Honor Vegas, baby, with a game night. Turn on the Tom Jones, cover the dining room table with green felt, and play poker or blackjack with a ten-dollar buy-in, or give everyone the same number of chips and hand out a prize to the big winners of the evening. It goes without saying that drinks are on the house. Send members off with a couple of lottery tickets so they can try their luck at home.

Slumber Party: Yeah, yeah, how juvenile. But acting out once in a while can help you regroup and take action. So try embracing your inner child for a night of pure girl bonding. You don't have to host an actual sleepover (although that would be totally rad), but ask members to wear their favorite pajamas or comfiest sweats. Queue the hits of various teen idols, then dance, get crazy, braid one another's hair, play truth or dare. Pig out on junk food or set up a sundae bar for women to make their own confection concoctions. And regarding the meeting itself, lay some blankets down and sit in a circle as you move efficiently and playfully through the business at hand.

Outdoor Themes

All-American Picnic: Channel your inner patriot and festoon your yard with all things red, white, and blue. Kick off the meeting with a reading of the Bill of Rights or your favorite amendment. Gather around a picnic table and serve up hot dogs and apple pie. Wave sparklers or American flags as you get down to John Philip Sousa.

Beach Blankets? Bingo!: Play a bit of old-school bingo to get things started. Lay beach towels around the yard (or even the living room), hand out small samples of sunscreen, brimmed hats, and beach bags (you could even create a club design and use an iron-on transfer to decorate each bag), and conduct your meeting while soaking up some rays. Serve sun tea and Popsicles to cool things down.

Luau—Aloha!: While you might not be able to jet off to the Big Island with your group, you can bring a bit of the South Pacific to your backyard. Light up some tiki torches and "lei" guests, or tuck a fresh flower behind an ear as they arrive. Skip roasting up a pig and making poi; instead, serve mai tais and daiquiris (with paper umbrellas, of course), along with fresh pineapple and mango.

Theme of the Week: Depending on what book or movie you're discussing or watching, why not match the snacks and decor to the theme? For example, if you are reading or watching The Great Gatsby, think Art Deco. Serve flutes of champagne, decorate in shades of black-and-white, play some Cole Porter tunes, and hand out a cool party favor like a sleek black journal for keeping book or film notes. The wine club Divas Uncorked usually pairs a wine theme (such as rosés) with an overall theme (such as In the Pink) for its monthly dinner parties.

HANDOUTS

Every gal likes a "free gift with purchase," and similarly, women like to be given materials at meetings, whether they are fun, informative, or a little bit of both. For your book or movie club, consider handing out rating cards or questionnaires. This will spark conversation and serve as a record of what you liked and disliked as a group. You could even collect everyone's answers and place them in a binder for future reference.

But it's not all about fun and games. Handing out instructional and informative hard copies to your craft club (as an example) will keep up members' interest level, along with their desire to improve their skills. Education is an important part of every dinner meeting for the Divas Uncorked. "We are very sophisticated about matching wine and food, but we still have to provide education. We send members home with a packet each month," says member Callie Crossley. Providing information about your financial group's stock performances and about investments the group is considering is key to keeping everyone in your group up-to-date. But also consider giving out information about a new market you're interested in, or even a sheet of terms it would be helpful to know. If you belong to a weekly poker night, print out some strategies on bluffing or betting, or lists of online poker Web sites you recently discovered. Members of your cycling club would appreciate that information you just picked up from your trainer about increasing stamina or eating properly before a long ride. If you are interested in something, chances are you constantly seek out information pertaining to its every facet. So share that info with your fellow members.

HANDOUTS FOR VARIOUS TYPES OF GROUPS:

Financial Club (investment, budgeting, finance): research on various stocks, list of Fortune 500 companies, articles on female-friendly companies

Book Club: book reviews, transcripts of interviews with various authors

Culture Club (movies, art, theater, music, TV): reviews, essays, sociological studies of the effects of media on society, score cards for rating a show or performance

Career Club (networking, life coaching): personality tests, networking "trees," goal questionnaires, research on different fields and markets

Gaming Group (cards, bingo, board games, casino outings): rules for a new game, strategies for winning, lists of the odds of various games

Craft Circle (knitting, quilting, scrapbooking, beading and jewelry making, journaling, needlepoint, crochet, candle making): instructions on a new technique, suggestions for a group project, directory of local or national craft stores, announcement of a new book release, list of helpful Web sites/reading materials

Interest Club (cooking, writing, wine tasting, travel, bird-watching): essays, articles, press clippings, blank journals for notes, step-by-step instructions for new techniques

Sporting Club: instructions for a new exercise, scientific studies regarding metabolism, body mass index, heart rate chart

Activist or Emotional Support Group: information on new legislation, politicians' biographies, numbers or addresses for petitioning or voicing support, daily affirmation, inspirational articles about individual courage or strength

Spiritual Gathering (Bible study, meditation, Kabbalah, Wicca, Buddhism, divination): prayers or intentions, information about different cultures or faiths, tips for meditation, historical research

Spa Party: at-home spa recipes, information on homeopathic remedies, properties of natural ingredients, massage techniques, aromatherapy and color-therapy charts

REFRESHMENTS

It's relatively easy to put together some satisfying snacks for your crowd. Cheese and crackers, a bunch of grapes, and a bit of salami will appease the most rabid pack of women. Then there are the standards of chips and dip, chips and salsa, cookies, and assorted chocolates.

But if you have time for more than a trip to the corner store, you can zest up your gathering with some truly unique and scrumptious snacks.

The first thing to do is to ferret out any special dietary needs that members may have and to work with them or around them as necessary. Any vegetarians in the group? Does anyone keep kosher? Is there a diabetic with a sweet tooth in the crowd? And now that you think about it, didn't Caroline refuse a carrot stick because she was on Atkins induction last month? It is a challenge to wade through the variety of women's tastes and diets, but think of it as an opportunity to try a few different recipes or dishes and to show your friends that you care about their needs.

Aside from your friends' diets, you should consider the type of group you have and the activities you'll be doing during the gathering. If you belong to a knitting circle or quilting bee, make sure your snacks aren't messy and your drinks won't stain your materials. If you are hosting your book club, again, you might want to serve neat finger food and a clear beverage. For your film club's movie night you'll want to provide snacks members can easily maneuver in the dark. Poker night? Make sure gamers' fingers aren't greasy—serve things on toothpicks! Of course, if you belong to a culinary club, you'll want to get your game on and cook up a storm.

Debra Lande's mah-jongg club takes its food as seriously as its game. "The host has to provide dinner. I was terrified because I didn't entertain that much. Having five people over at 6:30 on a workday seemed overwhelming. For about eight years, I wasn't happy about it. I served pizza and salad with a purchased dessert," Debra says. "Gail (another member) is the queen of takeout. You can't tell she didn't make it. I always wind up with two salads that are exactly alike, or everything is white. Now, I make something the night before or leave work early. And we know everyone's food preference: chicken or fish, lots of fruit things, but not chocolate because someone's allergic."

You'll need something to wash down all your tasty snacks. A couple of bottles of red and white wine are a fail-safe option, but also stock nonalcoholic beverages (iced tea, hot tea, coffee, soft drinks, and sparkling water) for teetotalers and pregnant or nursing women. And think about serving up a special punch or signature cocktail. That way, you don't need to worry about stocking a full bar or selecting a wine worthy of your group's resident oenophile.

For a Saturday or Sunday afternoon meeting, consider serving tea, scones, chocolates, and tea sandwiches—making sure to cut off the crusts! For a blustery night's gathering, provide mulled wine, rum-laced cider, hot toddies, or Irish coffees to warm up and rev up. For a balmy summer evening, hold the meeting outside and mix up mai tais servedwith little umbrellas.

Here are a few dishes and snacks that are easy to make and neat to eat:
- crudités and dip: crab, French onion, dill, and/or spinach-artichoke
- beef or chicken satay
- veggie or fruit kebobs
- shrimp cocktail
- guacamole, salsa, and blue-corn chips
- nuts or candied nuts
- Chex mix
- seasoned popcorn (for a movie club)
- popcorn balls
- small packages of licorice, Junior Mints, and other movie candy
- cheese plate with fruit slices, dried fruit, and crackers
- hard salami and prosciutto with a crusty bread
- bruschetta
- homemade pizza or pizza from store-bought dough (Trader Joe's, Pillsbury)
- sundaes (from a do-it-yourself sundae bar)

- tacos (from a do-it-yourself taco bar)
- deviled eggs
- olives stuffed with gorgonzola

Don't forget a few beverages to punch up a meeting:
- smoothies
- milk shakes (have a milk shake bar)
- cosmopolitans
- mulled wine
- rum-laced cider
- hot toddies
- Irish coffees
- eggnog (for the holidays)
- tea (serve high tea)
- various coffees (have a coffee bar if you have an espresso machine)

If you are having a slumber party, holiday party, or some occasion

---

FISH-HOUSE PUNCH

Mix the following ingredients:

> 1 cup plain sugar syrup (To make, heat 1 cup sugar and 1 cup water until well combined and until no sugar remains. Let cool.)
>
> 1½–2 cups fresh lemon juice
>
> 6¼ cups (approximately 1½ liters) Jamaican medium rum
>
> 3 cups (approximately 750 milliliters) brandy
>
> 1 cup peach brandy (or peach schnapps)
>
> Optional: 3 cups strong brewed tea (Lipton, for example)

For each quart of the above mixture, add 3 bottles of champagne. If it still tastes too strong, an extra bottle of champagne will "lighten" it up a bit without affecting the taste. Serving the punch in a punch bowl that has been prepared well in advance with an ice ring will keep the punch cold throughout the entire meeting or party. Freeze fruit in the ice ring to make it extra fancy!

Serves 35–50

---

where no one is planning on driving, try a spiked punch. This one comes from Jared Von Arx, an honorary member of a Philadelphia culture club. (As you can see from the ingredients, this is not for the weak of heart.) Legend has it that this punch was created in the eighteenth century at Pennsylvania's State Fishing and Social Club, hence its name.

Take a tip from the Divas Uncorked: the wine club recommends seeking out female-friendly businesses. In Boston, club members frequent Best Cellars (www.bestcellars.com), where you can identify wine by eight different characteristics—such as juicy, sweet, soft, or luscious—or by price or region. The business makes wine inviting, even to the beginner. The Divas list their many friends and partners on their Web site (www.divasuncorked.com), often giving them the Divas Uncorked stamp of approval.

Potlucks and Such

If the members of your group tend to contribute food and beverages at each meeting, so much the better! Meeting after work can present challenges for a hostess. Takeout is one option, but asking other members to bring something can be a better solution. Even then, it's nice to take into account everyone's time constraints and work situations. Take a tip from the Art Night group in Philadelphia and play to everyone's strengths and schedules. The group met for years every Monday night to work on group and individual art projects.

"We always found the problems with meeting after work were—one— we were hungry and—two—there's only so much time to meet, and we wanted to maximize our art time," artist e Bond says. "You can't spend the whole time eating, but you are going to be hungry. A lot of the food is takeout, or each person brings one thing, but the challenge is to bring a dish that can be made ahead of time, can be refrigerated at work until it is time for the meeting, or can even go unrefrigerated. Members with stressful jobs bring wine and bread, something they can pick up easily. And on days when *everyone's* beat, we just order pizza."

Don't fault a member if she always brings a store-bought dip and a bag of chips. The fact that she's committed to coming and bringing something demonstrates her commitment to the group. If you are underwhelmed by the sight of yet another bag of Doritos, give her a specific shopping list. Ask her to bring store-bought guacamole (or a few soft avocados), a red onion, and a lime, so the guacamole can be doctored up at the meeting. But if she never steps foot into a kitchen or decent grocery store, for goodness' sake don't ask her to select a wine or make a dish, however simple it may seem to you. Instead, ask her to grab two pints of Ben & Jerry's or a couple of packages of Pepperidge Farm cookies at the convenience store on her way to the meeting. You could even ask her to bring a few CDs and take care of the background music if you really would rather she focus her talents elsewhere.

If one member is coming straight from work and refrigeration is a challenge, suggest she make or purchase in advance cookies, brownies, a cake, or a pie—assuming that she can transport the item carefully.

Of course, someone can always bring a pound of freshly ground coffee, a couple of bottles of decent wine, some microbrewed beer, a few types of soda, or even some sparkling water to the meeting.

Here's another tip from the Divas Uncorked, regarding hangover prevention. (You know those girl-group meetings can get out of hand!) Drink water between meals or glasses of wine (keep a glass of water by the bed for nighttime hydration); take two aspirin before bed; and eat a banana upon waking (the starchiness will help burn off the alcohol).

ENTERTAINMENT

Unless you belong to a music or dance club, you don't want the music to distract you from your meeting. Select some mellow CDs or put together a playlist on your iPod in advance of the meeting. Advance prep will allow you to relax and will eliminate variables that may pull you away from a spirited group discussion.

Here are a few tried-and-true playlists I've put together for various gatherings. If you have an iPod or another digital audio player but don't have the songs in your music library, you can always purchase them online at iTunes or another music site for about a dollar per song. And many of these artists' CDs are fabulous on their own. Put a few into your stereo and just press *Shuffle*.

Mellow Mixes

The following mixes are perfect for a book club, craft circle, financial group, or spa party.

Chill Out

Leave the cares of the world behind, with some blues and mellow rock.

"Love Yourself," Zero 7

"You Can Love Yourself," Keb Mo

"Come Away with Me," Norah Jones

"Moondance," Van Morrison

"More than One Kind of Love," Joan Armatrading

"Wonderwall," Ryan Adams

"Crazy," Patsy Cline

"Soul Searchin'," Solomon Burke

"Ice Cream," Sarah McLachlan

"Unpretty," TLC

"Lost Cause," Beck

"Summertime," Fantasia

"Basement Apt.," Sarah Harmer

"Hallelujah," Jeff Buckley

"Keys to Your Love," Rolling Stones

"Slowly Surely," Jill Scott

"She Will Be Loved," Maroon 5

Veg Out

Choose this mix if you're all ready to unwind, but not if you have work to accomplish. It will put everyone in the mood for bed—it's that relaxing.

"I Wish I Was the Moon," Neko Case

"Satellite," Dave Matthews

"Skylark," k.d. lang

"Fast as I Can," Erin McKeown

"Blue in Green," Miles Davis

"Between Two Worlds," Shawn Colvin

"Part of the Process," Morcheeba

"Didn't I (Blow Your Mind This Time)," the Delfonics

"Sexual Healing," Ben Harper

"Appletree," Erykah Badu

"Body and Soul," Billie Holiday

"Prelude: La Fille aux Cheveux de Lin," Andrés Segovia

"Lush Life," John Coltrane and Johnny Hartman

"By Your Side," Sade

"Simple Things," Zero 7

"Girl from Ipanema," Stan Getz

Energy Mixes

Try the following mixes for a gaming group or cooking club. This music is zesty and up-tempo, but make sure it's kept to a moderate volume—unless the group asks you to blast it so they can rock out.

Swing Out, Sister!

Obviously, you can put on any Bobby Darin or Rat Pack CD to get the joint jumping, but here's a sampling if you want to mix up your playlist old-school-Vegas style.

"I Get a Kick Out of You," Frank Sinatra

"That Old Black Magic," Louie Prima

"I Don't Like You," Nightcaps

"Too Much," Elvis Presley

"Mr. Heat Miser," Big Bad Voodoo Daddy

"Please Don't Talk about Me When I'm Gone," Billie Holiday

"I Say a Little Prayer," Aretha Franklin

"More," Bobby Darin

"Ac-cent-tchu-ate the Positive," Bing Crosby

"Cosmopolitans," Erin McKeown

"Ain't That a Kick in the Head," Dean Martin

"Zoot Suit Riot," Cherry Poppin' Daddies

"That's Right," Lyle Lovett

"Son of a Preacher Man," Dusty Springfield

"Have You Met Miss Jones?," Robbie Williams

"Big Spender," Shirley Bassey

Girl Power

Sometimes, girls just wanna have fun, and this mix is sure to bring out the riot grrrls within all of you.

"Hands Clean," Alanis Morissette

"Toxic," Britney Spears

"Just Like a Pill," Pink

"Respect," Aretha Franklin

"32 Flavors," Ani Difranco

"No Scrubs," TLC

"Goodbye," Goodness

"Goodbye to You," Scandal

"If I Fall You're Going Down with Me," Dixie Chicks

"Why Can't I?," Liz Phair

"He Thinks He'll Keep Her," Mary Chapin Carpenter

"Hammer and Nail," Indigo Girls

"Louise," Beth Amsel

"Come a Long Way," Michelle Shocked

"Any Man of Mine," Shania Twain

"All You Wanted," Michelle Branch

"This Town Is Wrong," The Nields

Heat It Up

Consider kicking things up by kicking up your heels at the beginning or end of a meeting with these tried-and-true dance tunes. Just *try* to keep from moving.

"Yeah!," Usher

"Real World," Matchbox 20

"I Don't Like You," Nightcaps

"Get Free," The Vines

"Musicology," Prince

"Annie Get Your Gun," Squeeze

"Ray of Light," Madonna

"Get Ur Freak On," Missy Elliott

"Love Rollercoaster," Ohio Players

"Satisfaction," Rolling Stones

"Sick of Myself," Matthew Sweet
"She's a Beauty," Tubes
"The Way You Move," Outkast
"God Is a DJ," Pink
"Wherever You Will Go," The Calling
"Tilt Ya Head Back," Nelly and Christina Aguilera

Rock Out

Again, this is guaranteed to make your members dance, nod in time to the music, lip-synch, or a combination of all three.

"I'm Every Woman," Chaka Khan
"Rock Steady," Aretha Franklin
"Fever," Madonna
"Everyday I Write the Book," Elvis Costello and the Attractions
"Move Away," Boy George
"Like I Love You," Justin Timberlake
"Crazy in Love," Béyonce
"Devil's Haircut," Beck
"Hey Mama," Black Eyed Peas
"Poison Arrow," ABC
"Extraordinary," Liz Phair
"Tenderness," General Public
"I'm a Slave 4 U," Britney Spears
"Endicott," Kid Creole & the Coconuts
"This Love," Maroon 5
"Hey Jealousy," Gin Blossoms
"Mesolithic," Eddie from Ohio

Guest Stars

If you have a special guest attending your meeting, make sure to let members know about it in advance. It may give the group extra incentive to be prepared and on time. Distribute handouts in advance or at the meeting so members are briefed and have questions or comments ready for the guest. And don't forget to ask the speaker if there are any materials he or she would like you to give to the group.

Make sure your guest has directions. If she is traveling a significant distance, book the flight, rent the car, and make hotel accommodations. If you can pay for it all in advance, do so. The easier you can make her journey, the better her experience. Make sure you tell her to keep receipts so you can reimburse her promptly.

Of course, your guest might be local, and happy to make a free house call. If so, lucky you. When he arrives, take his coat, introduce him to the rest of the members (if the group is a modest number), lead him to a comfortable chair, offer him a drink, and make him feel as relaxed as you can. Don't rush into the evening's discussion until he's had a chance to catch his breath and collect his thoughts.

After the meeting, follow up with a thank-you note or phone call. You never know when you might want to invite a guest back! See pages 113–116 for more information on finding and booking guests for your group.

PARTY FAVORS

You love your girls. You want to show them how much they mean to you (and—let's be honest—what a spectacular and thoughtful hostess you are). So when it's your turn to host the group, put together a party favor or small gift bag.

But what's appropriate and how can you avoid breaking the bank?

Remember, it's the thought that counts. You don't need to buy Tiffany tag bracelets for everyone (although I'm sure they'd appreciate it). Instead, buy small gifts they'll be touched by that won't make them feel obligated to reciprocate when it's time for them to host the group. Cool pocket calculators would be perfect for your investment group, hand-crafted or personalized bookmarks for your book club, lanolin lotion or skeins of yarn from your stash for your knitting circle. Part of a hiking club? Hand out pedometers, local trail maps, or some homemade gorp.

And here are a few more ideas for group-specific gifts:

Financial Club: checkbook cover, money clip, change purse, piggy bank

Book Club: paperback book covers, bookmarks, Post-its for marking juicy passages

Culture Club: movie guidebook, movie passes, opera glasses, comedy/tragedy charm, *Variety* magazine, movie poster

Career Club: business-card holder, cool clipboard, fancy paperclips, notebook, gel pen, wooden foot massager

Gaming Group: deck of cards, fuzzy dice, travel bingo, slot-machine key chain, mini board game, crossword book, lottery tickets

Craft Circle: tote bag, craft tools or materials, hand lotion, photo album or notebook to document craft projects, hand massager

Interest Club: (depends on the type of group) tipping chart, cooking utensil, spices, seeds, small herb plant, and so on

Sporting Club: thermal socks, pedometer, baseball cap, water bottle, snack bars, trail mix, sunscreen

Activist or Emotional Support Group: Kleenex, small book of affirmations, stationery, phone card, statement pin, bumper sticker, bubble bath

Spiritual Gathering: crystal, prayer book, rosary, patron saint charm, book of saints, CD of soothing sounds, tarot cards

Spa Party: samples of lotions and potions, nail file, foot scrub, sponge or loofah, eye mask, ponytail holders, candle

EVENT PLANNING

Maybe you never envisioned yourself as a party planner, but if your group meets at a restaurant or bar you may find yourself an ad hoc event coordinator. See Chapter 7: Growing Pains & Gains for tips on hosting an event off-site (i.e., somewhere other than your living room).

Hosting should never feel like a chore. If you put thought and care into planning, you will be as enthusiastic wining and dining your members as they will be gathering in your welcoming home.

CHAPTER 5

Policing the Ranks

The path to true girl-group love never did run smooth, so why should your club be any different? As much as your members adore (or at least tolerate) one another, someone will inevitably act out. A member may suddenly drop out of sight for several meetings without so much as a phone call. Or she may hog the conversation, not letting other members get a word in edgewise and dismissing their points when they do. Or there may be a couple of members who seem to go at each other by the end of every gathering.

What's up with these people? Why can't we all just get along?

Well, not everyone can be the responsible, sociable, perfectly agreeable woman you are—yeah right. You know that you, too, have your off days, when you need your club to cut some you slack or offer support. But where does a group draw the line?

Like it or not, you must patrol your group, however subtly, and from time to time deal with a member (sometimes yourself) either privately or en masse. It's helpful to be prepared.

A FEW COMMON CASE STUDIES

As your group settles into itself, chances are members will become comfortable (i.e., complacent) and will allow their true tendencies to emerge. For example, you might be very opinionated but may tamp down your urge to pipe in on every comment during your first few investment-club meetings. After a while, however, when everyone seems to get along and you consider everyone good friends, you feel perfectly fine jumping in to the conversation whenever you have a point to make—which is, on average, every thirty seconds. Other club members, who like you (most of the time) and who are polite, are probably quiet suffering your new insufferable personality.

Don't let this happen to you.

Nip obnoxious behavior in the bud before it has a chance to take root and choke the fun and energy out of your club. Here are a few ideas for addressing some common problems, but feel free to put your own spin on the situation. You have to do what you feel most comfortable with. If you're nonconfrontational, a heartfelt letter might get the point across without making you break out in a nasty rash. If you—and your club members—are straight shooting, tell the offending member to get it together, as soon as she misbehaves. No reason to stew over the problem and possible solutions when club members share a straightforward attitude. Just to cover all the bases, here are some tips for keeping all sorts of bad behavior at bay.

If one member is a motormouth:
- Use a timer so each member gets an equal opportunity to talk.
- Establish a rule that you will all take turns speaking.
- Redirect the conversation: address other members and ask pointed questions of them.
- Designate a code word or phrase (unusual ones like Lilliputian or prehensile tail grab everyone's attention) for use when someone gets out of hand.
- Get up and ask the chatty Cathy for help in bringing out snacks/drinks.
- If this member is you: Ask one woman in the club to give you a signal when you get motormouthed.

"We have a mom who's not always at the meeting, but when she is, she always has something to say," says Mocha Moms L.A. president Sherry Petrie. "We listen. We tell members that if you make a suggestion, you own the project. And/or if you haven't been here, don't come in here with negativity and running your mouth. Come in with a solution."

Carol Hamlin chooses to be laid-back when someone in her Bible-study group is running at the mouth; other members are not so laissez-faire. "One woman talks too much and is completely oblivious to the fact. Another member has decided to 'manage' her. It's interesting to watch her body language when the woman starts going on and on. She gets real stiff in her chair and you can almost see her thinking, 'Oh, here she goes again.' She interrupts the woman and starts talking over her. She tries to get the conversation going in a different direction, and get the other women in the group to go along with this. It doesn't work very well," Carol says with more than a touch of bemusement.

If members talk over one another:
- Ask someone a question, addressing her by name. For example, "Jane, can you update us on next month's guest speaker?" Using a name will give all the women pause.
- Tell the group to pipe down—if everyone has a healthy ego.
- Adhere to agendas and give the floor to one member at a time. If someone interrupts, the rest of the group should feel free to chide the offender. She won't want to be embarrassed twice.
- Blow a whistle to get everyone's attention when they are out of control.
- If this member is *you*: Try taking a deep breath every time you want to speak. It will slow and calm you down.

Since none of the Divas Uncorked members are particularly reticent, they find themselves all talking at once during meetings. Because they are so forthright, they just say "shut up" if someone's talking too much. It works for them. If you have a group of women with pretty thick skin, it may work for them too.

If one member is *always* late:
- Start on time, every time, no matter who's missing.
- Charge money for tardiness or other infractions, and put it into a general pool toward a retreat or another worthy cause.
- Call her on the carpet when she arrives. She won't want to be publicly dressed down again.
- Suggest carpooling so that another woman picks up the offending member up in a timely fashion.
- Allocate the first fifteen minutes or half hour to socializing so she doesn't miss anything and the group doesn't become irritated. Maria Young's Grand Rapids book club uses the time to catch up on neighborhood news.

"We talk about strangers approaching kids in the neighborhood, what's going on with our kids' lives, how do I get my son into spring baseball, as well as share household tips about what takes out different kinds of stains, for example. And there's always husband bashing," Maria says.

- If this member is *you:* Stop it! Tardiness isn't a winning quality. Set an alarm on your cell phone or PDA, move the meeting's time up by half an hour in your datebook, ask someone to pick you up—just do whatever's necessary to show up on time.

Debra Lande was the tardy one in her mah-jongg group for a while. Her friends didn't like it. "One day I was really late and they confronted me, and I walked out and said, 'I can't take the pressure. I quit.' I realized something was wrong with my job and resolved it in within a few weeks," Debra says. "Meanwhile, I got letters from the women in the group, who made some really good points. Until then, I didn't know what it meant to be in a group. It seemed like just another obligation and a stupid game. I looked at my life and figured out why I was so reactive. I liked the community a lot and decided to go back after a month. It's worth it to me to be with this group of people."

If one member is routinely negative or depressed:

- Suggest she seek professional help (your club should not function as a place for her to air her issues, unless of course, it's a social therapy group).
- Keep the focus on the group's interests and off her and her woes.
- Ask her opinion on a light or fun topic to keep her mind more agreeably occupied.
- Ask her what's wrong. After she answers and you offer a bit of encouragement or advice, switch the subject. She may just need to feel heard and supported.
- Ignore her bad attitude. She may sulk to garner your attention. Don't derail the group by indulging her petulance.
- If this member is *you:* If you recognize that you are a pill or always blue, you might want to see a therapist. Don't rely on your club to be a sounding board for your woes. That's probably not why you put it together or joined

it in the first place. If you don't feel you need professional help, try getting together with a friend outside of the club to talk about your problems so you can put them on the shelf during meetings.

Sometimes people just need to be around other people. A woman may need the group without expecting any special attention. "We have one woman struggling with depression, but she doesn't inflict it on us. We know she's down because she's so quiet. If she didn't show up, then we'd be really worried," Carol Hamlin says about a member of her Bible-study group.

And sometimes members are as comfortable with one another as they would be with family, so they just let it rip. The trick is that when one member feels comfortable enough to say something negative, another should be equally comfortable saying that her attitude isn't acceptable. "Two members have known each other for thirty years," Debra Lande says about her San Francisco mah-jongg group. One says something cutting and the other is able to say, 'That's not OK.'"

If two members hate each other:
- Tell them both to resolve their differences or leave the group.
- Give them separate assignments or tasks that keep them away from each other.
- Seat them far apart during meetings.
- Refuse to listen to complaints from either of them about the other—you can't play favorites, and triangulation is deadly to relationships and to your group.
- If one of these members is *you*: Decide if your dislike for the woman is more important than your love of the group. If it's not, find a way to tolerate her so you don't completely throw off the energy of the meetings.

Sherry Petrie called out this bad behavior to her Mocha Moms L.A. chapter. "Two moms were getting into it with each other, and it got out into the group's e-mail. How do you work that out when you have a relationship with both moms? One member wanted to talk, and the other was angry and hostile and didn't want to have anything to do with her. I wrote a full-page letter to the entire group saying that I understand personality differences but this can't happen again, because it damages the group." The feuding members did end up talking to each other and working out their grievances. "They basically said, 'I respect you enough to respect you to disagree.' Now, if I hear things in someone's tone in an e-mail, I think OK, you're having a *day*. If I catch that, I call them and see if they're OK," Sherry says. Taking a proactive approach at the first hint of discontent is an excellent way to head off a full-out war.

If one member acts like Boss Hogg:

- If the women in your group all have strong personalities, just tell the domineering member to chill out whenever she oversteps her bounds.
- Delegate, delegate, delegate. Different members should have responsibility over different club concerns. If one member wants to run roughshod over the entire group, give her complete authority over one specific area.
- Give in and let her do everything. Enjoy the benefits of the group without any of the work.
- If this member is *you*: Do you want another full-time job? Do you want to resent the club and all the members? Do you like being a martyr? If you answered yes to any or all of these questions, you're nuts. As soon as you feel you've overcommitted yourself, delegate or ask for assistance. If you wanted to do everything yourself, you wouldn't need a club or group, right? If you don't trust anyone else to do it right, show the other members how. It may take more time initially to train them, but it will pay off in the long run. And when something needs to be done, pause and really think about all that it will involve before raising your hand. Think of your short-term and long-term schedule. Can you honestly fit this in, or will you end up feeling completely stressed out? And wouldn't it be better to let someone else do the task at hand so you could focus your talents on a more suitable project? After quickly cycling through these questions, if you still want to volunteer, go for it.

If one member has completely checked out:

- Recognize that she may come to the group to escape her busy life. If your group isn't a spa party or nap advocacy organization, come armed with questions to engage her and spark her interest.

- Ply her with caffeine, light snacks, and a chilly room to keep her alert (old-school classroom tricks). Warn others to eat beforehand and to bring a sweater.
- Ask her what she gets out of the group. If she's not interested any longer, it would be best for everyone if she left the group, no hard feelings.
- If this member is *you:* Make sure you get enough sleep the night before the meeting and that you leave your other worries at the door. Drink something with caffeine, sniff peppermint (a natural stimulant), pinch yourself, sit in an uncomfortable chair, and do your best to pay attention. And just know that the malaise will eventually pass. In the meantime, stifle your yawns and try to stay alert. It's the polite thing to do.

If club members start splintering into cliques:
- Realize that this is bound to happen, and embrace the fact that some members get along swimmingly.
- Delegate small tasks to or create committees of two or three members who don't normally socialize.
- Make sure the meeting space is set up for group conversation rather than for small cliques. If it is a group that meets at small tables, play musical chairs regularly to mix things up.
- Be a formal hostess: put place cards at the table(s), or show each member to her seat.
- If part of the problem is *you:* It's natural to like some members more than others. But if you want to socialize with certain women, do it outside of group meetings, and try your best not to talk about the group when you get together. Use the meetings as a chance to catch up with the other women.

If one member feels shunned or left out:
- Ask her to take charge of some area of responsibility—be it food, event planning, fund-raising, or Web site development—and tell her how perfect she is for the job.
- Make a point of sitting next to her during a meeting or chatting with her before or after the gathering.
- If she was accidentally left off an e-mail list or overlooked in some way, apologize for the mistake, and take care not to repeat the error.

- If this member is *you:* Be proactive and volunteer for a project. E-mail group members between meetings. The more you contribute to the group, the more you'll get out of it. If you feel you're being deliberately shunned, privately ask a member you feel close to her opinion on the matter. If there's something the group is unhappy about, it's better to know so you can address the situation.

If one member is rigid about rules and procedures:
- Be aware that if everyone else is drinking or laid-back to begin with and she is a teetotaling, type-A personality, chances are that she'll be wound up like a pocket watch during the meeting, trying to keep everyone and everything on track. Try allocating downtime to part of the meeting, even going so far as to put it on the agenda. She can't argue if you are sticking to the agenda!
- Ignore her sour mood.
- Take her aside and tell her that the socializing and camaraderie are equally as important as taking care of all the month's action items.

Take into consideration a member's frame of reference and frame of mind when dealing with a single-minded member. "One woman insisted we focus on one Bible study every single time we got together," Carol Hamlin says. "It infuriated her that we'd get off topic. Most of the women in the group are not so rigid about the Bible study. But this woman had been isolated from other women; she worked as a day care provider for twenty years and maybe didn't know how to play well with other adults. She was chronically depressed and dropped out of the group. The group obviously disappointed her in some way, and poof! She left."

If one member is *stressed:*
- Begin the meeting by doing some deep-breathing exercises or by giving one another short shoulder massages.
- Leave her be. She might just need a space to be quiet where no one expects anything from her for an hour.
- Ask her to help out in the kitchen. Chopping can be very therapeutic!
- Monitor her drinking. A glass or two of wine might take the edge off; four or five will just add to the problem.

It's bound to happen: one member loses it. Perhaps it's work or her health or a personal relationship that causes her to blow. That doesn't excuse her behavior, but it should elicit a sympathetic attitude from the group, at least for a meeting or two. "People go through a lot and, as friends, we try to help each other out. We'll flip months if a member has too much on her plate. It's necessary to help each other out—we are ten different women, with ten different schedules and lifestyles. Like sisters, we aren't going anywhere," says Divas Uncorked member Callie Crossley.

If one member tries to push her own agenda or business at meetings:

- Allocate fifteen minutes at the beginning or end of each meeting for members to make any announcements, either personal or professional.
- When a member starts to pitch her business, suggest she send an e-mail out to the group instead, since time is limited.
- Ask that no personal business be discussed at the meetings. Members can call one another individually.

Obviously some clubs, like the Divas Who Dine, are set up to promote members' businesses, but some structure still has to exist so that no one member ends up monopolizing the meeting. "This is a networking group intended to support each member's business and career," says founder and president Zoe Alexander. "We go around at every lunch and each woman has a minute to talk about what she is working on and what she might need: a DJ, event planners, florists, a printer, etc. Everyone's so eager to help each other. No shame here in self-promoting; my theory is that you have to put it out there to get any results."

Some women, however, might join a group just to push a business and might never contribute to the club, let alone show up for meetings. In this case, making attendance mandatory and requiring a project or two might help weed out the opportunists. "We have an application but no screening process, so mothers join who just want business from us," says Mocha Moms L.A. president Sherry Petrie. "So what we've done is let each member say what they do a few times a year, but [we] do not allow them to send e-mails on regular basis."

If one member consistently drops the ball:
- Give her long-term projects she can do on her own timetable.
- Pair members up on projects so partners hold each other responsible.
- Send out reminders to all members a couple days before an event or meeting.

"We keep each other accountable," Maria Young says of her church's moms' group. "It's easier to make calls when a group is smaller, and everyone knows if you mess up or drop the ball."

So basically, when trouble is a-brewin' in the ranks of your club, nip bad behavior in the bud and be kind about it. Setting up a dynamic where things are dealt with openly is a great way to avoid headaches and ill will. "We are one big family, and I make sure to nurture us all," says Mocha Moms L.A. president Sherry Petrie. "Of course, I end up pacifying a lot of these mothers, but I tell them 'I have five kids, I don't need another hundred.' We have some strong-willed sisters up in here, me being one of them. I've had to tell people that I'm not about to baby them. They say, 'OK, momma.' I respond, 'Do not do that. I am for real.'"

THE MONEY STRAIN

It's naive to expect that everyone will always pay dues, fees, and other expenses in a timely and fair fashion. Remember that each woman grew up with different parents with wildly disparate views on spending, saving, paying, and so on. Members' economic backgrounds and current financial statuses might also vary greatly.

The best advice I can offer is to be as clear and detailed about money as you can, and to be up front about it. Some people feel that they are being taken advantage of when an expense crops up after the fact. Be realistic when setting dues, and make your accounting records readily available to members.

It's also important to keep everyone accountable. Don't let someone slide unless you have a policy in place to do so. It can become time-consuming keeping track of and tracking down outstanding payments, and you can end up looking like a nag. If you make it clear from the beginning that late payments mean probation or expulsion from the group, members will treat finances seriously.

Sample Check Request

```
Date:
Member name:
Purpose of check:
Amount requested:
Make check payable to:
If reimbursement, please attach receipt. If not, please submit receipt
when transaction is completed.
When approved, reimbursements will be paid within thirty days.
Approved by:
President [initial]
Treasurer [initial]
```

And when it comes to giving members access to group funds, it's absolutely imperative that they submit a check request beforehand and provide receipts afterward. If members agree, avoid advances and check requests altogether, and reimburse them for expenses upon submission of receipts.

TOO MANY TYPE-A PERSONALITIES

A group of driven women in one room can be incredibly energizing. But it can also cause a few complications. You may get several stubborn women with very particular ideas butting heads over an issue. Often, type-A women trade tact for directness, and that can create animosity within the ranks.

On the flip side, candor can be refreshing and can cause latent feelings to be dealt with handily so everyone can move on with everything out in the open. Otherwise, resentment can fester and explode at a later date. If you apply a "what you see is what you get" approach to group dynamics, and everyone knows to voice their opinions and feelings, a member won't be tempted to read into what's said or what's not said.

Take a tip from Boston's Divas Uncorked wine club. Members are all very accomplished, take-charge, type-A women. To make this work in their favor, when a situation arises, members ask, "Who's the designee?" If they didn't do this, all the women in the club would step up to take care of business. This can overwhelm someone on the outside, as well as cause confusion within the group. Sometimes, though, a group can accomplish more together than its members can individually. To wit: One Diva was worried that she would have a problem returning some defective furniture. When the sales clerk saw the rest of the Divas standing in solidarity behind the customer he said, "No problem, ma'am." So use the power of your power girls to your advantage!

TOO MANY TYPE-B PERSONALITIES

Do you have the opposite problem? Do members lack the drive to get things done quickly or the desire to say what they mean or want? While type Bs can be patient and friendly, they can also be slow to act and passive-aggressive. If after carefully selecting members you still have a group that's predominantly passive, there are a few measures you can take.

First of all, delegation and agendas are essential to moving projects along. But with that must come accountability. You have to ask for status updates regularly, at meetings and by e-mail in between meetings. In short, you have to monitor.

While type-B personalities are purportedly laid-back, some things are bound to get under their skin. Members may tamp down negative emotions or frustrations and put on a happy face in an attempt to avoid unpleasantness. Sooner or later, however, they will crack, and the temporary unpleasantness they could have experienced will in fact be replaced by a nastiness that will be harder to forget. You've probably done this yourself—suppressed anger until it bubbles over and explodes in an uncontrolled rage.

This is not good.

If you sense dissatisfaction among one or more members, gently broach the subject individually and try to figure out the source of the problem. Being easygoing, your type-B member may make light of the issue, but if you employ a friendly tone and concerned prompting, she will mostly likely divulge her concerns.

If a member is unhappy about an aspect of the group, talk it out with her. Refer to the advice on pages 89–98 for solutions to common problems. She may just need someone to vent to, in a supportive and nonjudgmental environment.

TRIANGULATION, SOCIALIZING OUTSIDE OF THE GROUP

There will be some pockets of socializing outside of the group. Members have connections to one another and those connections will grow as a result of the group.

This is a good thing, really.

However, there may be insecure members who will take relationships between other members personally. This is—frankly—too bad. One member's insecurities are not your or your group's problem. That's not to say that you shouldn't be sensitive to that member's feelings, but do not try to conceal deepening friendships or outside-the-group get-togethers. Each woman will have to cope with different levels of friendship and preference in the group, much as she has to every day in the world.

But there are precautions you can take to make everyone feel valued and liked. Note that the smaller the club, the worse triangulation can be. If you only have five or six members, and one person feels left out, that can feel like real rejection because there's no one to turn to for friendship. This is an organized group(to some extent), more than a casual, impromptu gathering of friends, so it is each woman's responsibility to foster a convivial group atmosphere. Make a point to talk with each member separately at each gathering. In between meetings, send out individual e-mails to members so they feel singled out and special. Better yet, call them—even if it's just a five-minute call.

THE LAST RESORT

To put it bluntly, there may come a time when you have no choice but to kick someone out of the clubhouse. If the member has been simply falling down on the job, missing meetings and not doing her share of the work, this might be a painless conversation. You both might want to part ways. Problem solved.

However, if the offending member has been causing a different problem, such as getting belligerent at every meeting or absconding with club funds, you'll need to sit her down and give her her walking papers.

This won't be easy. Prepare for yelling, tears, pleading, and/or feelings of betrayal and surprise.

Making the decision to kick someone out should be done carefully and fairly. Do not act rashly and eject someone after one ugly meeting. Give the member a few meetings to redeem herself or confirm your feeling that she's out of place in your group. Privately poll members about your wish to oust the member, or if you are the club president and the rules give you the authority to do this yourself, take matters into your own hands. Either way, do not make this a group event, no matter how large or small your club. Ask the member to stay behind after a meeting, or meet with her in a neutral location (a short coffee break at a café is perfect). Be kind and be firm. Tell her that you value her friendship and everything she has brought to the group but that she is a bad fit. Say that you think the club and she will be happier if you went your separate ways. If she protests and asks for another chance, tell her that this was not a hasty decision and was made after observing the dynamic for several months or meetings. If she has done the group wrong, simply say that the group is revoking her membership and the decision is final.

Without drama or details, let your group know that the woman in question is no longer affiliated with your organization. While members should feel free to pursue a friendship with her, they should not disclose any details of club meetings or activities. While this may be obvious, it is still important to clearly let members know what is expected of them. The rejected member will most likely harbor ill will toward the group, and giving her any fodder for complaint could result in negative attention in the community. There's no way to avoid this being an uncomfortable situation but doing it with class and respect will hopefully ease the pain and be appreciated by the former member.

Perhaps you will have no need for the many suggestions in this chapter. If that's the case, please let us know where we can sign up for your group! Regardless of how smoothly your club runs or how swimmingly members get along, thinking in advance about troublesome dynamics and issues will go a long way toward ensuring that problems—large or small—can be dealt with handily. Don't let a sticky group dynamic or individual problem siphon energy and attention away from the work and play of your girl group!

CHAPTER 6

Staying Motivated

No matter how gung ho you and your friends start out, you are bound to hit a wall and lose momentum or enthusiasm. Sometimes a sunny attitude simply isn't enough to buoy your spirits and infuse your group with energy.

Relationships flag all the time, but the important thing is to stick things out and see the rough or boring patches through. Your girl group, too—with a bevy of relationships—is bound to flatline or become frustrating for a spell.

Accept that this will happen. Work to minimize the fallout.

To keep spirits and the interest level high, you'll need to mix things up in your club. Take field trips (they're not just for kids), bring in guests, embark on a group project, or just change the format of your meeting.

Spirits sag because of the weather, a bad day at work, a rude comment at the grocery store, and yes, because of the strain of group commitments. So your group has got to be not only rewarding but also downright fun, an escape from members' everyday lives. Something as small as a mass e-mail or a small gift can keep women jazzed about their membership in your club.

Rallying around a member in need, for instance, is a great way to keep the club enthusiasm soaring. The support group Mocha Moms L.A. puts together eight days' worth of meals for new moms and their families, just to give new mothers a rest. Traditions like this are wonderful for fostering camaraderie and support within the group.

Sometimes, however, you need more extreme measures to keep spirits soaring. Plan them out before enthusiasm has already waned.

DOWNERS THAT CAN AFFECT YOUR GROUP:

- dissent or discord within ranks
- members who are not pulling their weight
- scheduling challenges
- routine meetings
- dismal or noisy meeting places
- bad coffee or skimpy snacks (especially if members come straight from work without eating)
- poor weather conditions
- upsetting national or international news

DOWNERS THAT CAN AFFECT INDIVIDUAL MEMBERS:

- an overly ambitious schedule
- difficulties on the job
- money woes
- a troubled romantic relationship
- an unsatisfying sex life
- weight gain
- hormones
- a sick relative or pet
- ongoing home or car repair
- irksome neighbors

FIELD TRIPS

When it comes to field trips, there's no such thing as too much planning. Collect fees far in advance, set rendezvous times, make and double-check reservations, arrange for group transportation if possible (to ensure that everyone is present and accounted for), and be sure not to tire anyone out or go too long without food or water. Wear sunscreen. OK, people are obviously responsible for themselves, but it never hurts to pack an emergency kit with water, snacks, sunscreen, ibuprofen, bandages, and the like, so no one is brought low by a nasty cut or dehydration.

Take a deep breath and we'll break down the details of a field trip. Remember, field trips are fun!

First, pick your destination or activity. Will the location be suitable for your group? If your club is rather large, fitting into a cramped art gallery or crowding around a park ranger as he or she narrates a nature hike will be a challenge. Conversely, letting a huge group of women free in the city or at the zoo can result in someone getting lost or left behind. Employing the buddy system isn't a bad idea in such a case. Neither is splitting the group into two different excursions to keep the numbers down. Choosing two slightly different trips means members can elect the activity that most interests them. If your destination charges a fee, ask for a group discount. Don't be shy. Let the size of the group work for you.

It takes far more advance planning to host or attend an event out of town. Send payment ahead of time; some places will secure your reservation with a credit card imprint that isn't actually charged until the date of the event. Investigate this as a possibility.

If your group is small, things will be much easier. For most activities—be it an author's lecture on a book your group just completed, a museum visit, or a girls' night out at a dance club—it's no problem to plan for a dozen or so women. Even for small groups, however, call ahead and see if special arrangements (a private tour, a separate room, a group discount, and so on) can be made. If you have special interests or needs, make sure to voice them when you call. Whether it's a wheelchair for one member, a particular subject you'd like a docent to focus on during a tour, a certain park ranger you'd like to have leading a hike, time limitations, or dietary restrictions, organizations will do their best to accommodate your requests as long as they know about them well in advance.

Take into consideration the distance you will have to travel. If your destination is close by, you'll probably be able to drive separately or in small groups and not worry too much about transportation. If, however, it's farther away, you might want to explore public transportation or a rental van. And unless one member plans on doing all the driving, factor in rental insurance and fees for multiple drivers—let safety and prudence override frugality. Don't discount hiring a driver. Some car, cab, bus, and limo services have drivers available as chauffeurs. The drivers usually expect tips, so factor that expense in as well. Call around to find the transportation that best serves your needs.

CAR-RENTAL GUIDELINES

- Don't assume anything: ask the rental agency if it can also supply a driver.
- If you are already insured, you may not need to purchase rental insurance. But make certain that every potential driver is insured.
- Ask the customer service representative specific questions about the pick-up and drop-off time for the rental car. Even one extra hour can add considerably to the bill.
- Before you pile into the car, carefully inspect the exterior and interior for any damage to the vehicle.
- Fill up the gas tank before returning the car. It's much, much cheaper that way.

Field Trips, Outings, and Lectures—Oh My!

You think a field trip is a fine idea, but the question remains, what exactly should the group do? Well, the possibilities are as endless as your imagination and enthusiasm. Keep your eyes open for things related to your club's theme. For instance, Boston's Divas Uncorked wine club was able to attend a sneak preview of the wine-related indie film *Sideways*. Use the following list of possible outings as a starting point for brainstorming, either by yourself or with the entire group.

- *Financial Club:* budget workshop, investment seminar, stock exchange or board of trade tour, Securities and Exchange Commission tour, U.S. Mint tour

- *Book Club:* author reading, book fair, lecture, memoir-writing seminar, scrapbooking or bookbinding workshop, volunteering at children's story hour

- *Culture Club:* art fair, gallery opening, museum exhibition, concert, dance performance, film festival, movie premiere, music festival, poetry slam, behind-the-scenes theater tour, free outdoor theater, improvisation class, performance class, stand-up comedy class

- *Career Club:* career fair, management seminar, women's expo, lunch with a CEO, Myers-Briggs testing/analysis, presentation to students at local college

- *Gaming Group:* bingo night, local casinos, professional gambling lesson, Scrabble tournament, Las Vegas or Atlantic City trip

- *Craft Circle:* craft show, craft store workshop, folk art exhibition, yarn expo, craft-related TV-program screening

- *Interest Club:* bartending class, cooking workshop to learn specific technique or cuisine, dance lesson, flower show, factory tour, nature walk, travel lecture or slide show, wine tasting at winery or tasting room

- *Sporting Club:* group session with trainer; road trip to new location for biking, running, skating, rock climbing, etc.; volunteering at a professional race or game

- *Activist or Emotional Support Group:* lecture, protest, rally, governmental hearing or meeting, spiritual service, playdate at the playground

- *Spiritual Gathering:* psychic or tarot reading, recital or concert at church, tour of cathedral, visit to different religious services

- *Spa Party:* outdoor park, private yoga class, massage workshop, department store makeovers with visiting makeup artists

The sky's the limit. Just keep your eyes peeled for anything that may be relevant to your group. Sometimes the trip will be a no-brainer (taking your hiking club for a climb in the nearby mountains) and sometimes it will be more of a stretch (taking your craft club to a big flower show for inspiration). Regardless of the destination, the Divas Uncorked wine club advises, know your group. Think about whether all the members are up for roughing it or whether it's better to splurge on a truly indulgent experience. For their week in Napa, the Divas rented a house. "We don't do rustic," says Callie emphatically. "Our group comes by its name." It wasn't just any house: it was a five-bedroom house in a gated community. Members woke up to hot-air balloons outside their windows. The following year they went to Sonoma, and the house was even more posh. It had a pool and individual casitas. The Divas hired a chef for one night. They rented vans and had each member take a turn as the designated driver. Down the road, they plan to fit into one car so no one misses anything (meaning outrageous comments, girl talk, and gossip).

RETREATS

Since a cross-country bonding experience with your whole group piled into in a car and hitting the open road is probably impractical, the next best thing is a group retreat. Getting away for the weekend or longer (and getting away from the responsibilities of home and work) is an excellent way to do some hard-core connecting in a short amount of time.

Follow the same procedure you would for a shorter field trip, researching locations, accommodations, and transportation, and coming up with an agenda—even if it's loose—for the getaway. Beach houses, lakefront cottages, and mountain cabins are all fabulous rentals and can really take you and your club away from everyday worries. If that's not possible, renting out a few rooms in town at a nice hotel and unplugging for the weekend will serve a similarly indulgent purpose.

Use your members and their connections. One woman might have a family vacation place that's available. Through her professional contacts, another woman might be able to score you an amazing deal at a resort. "Barb has a beach house in Delaware that she shares with her brother, so she started having Art Night retreats in the summer. Everyone drives down and spends the weekend. We put tables on an outdoor enclosed porch and one member teaches us something, and the rest of the time we work on our own stuff," artist e Bond says of her Philadelphia art group. One weekend, the group scheduled poorly and Barb's niece—a dancer—

showed up with two friends. They all wound up joining in and making stuff when they weren't dancing on the beach. Now the two groups plan on meeting at the house for a joint retreat. The more the merrier!

The weekend shouldn't be all about club business, however. The Art Night members take turns making huge dinners; they drink wine, watch movies, and read books that will inspire them. As e Bond says, "Any place can be a place for art." But it's a whole lot easier when the sound you hear is not a cell phone ringing but the waves crashing against the shore.

As relaxing and mellow as a retreat sounds, there are still tasks to be divvied up or shared. Perhaps it's the vacation spirit of the event, but division of labor often seems to happen naturally. Some women will want to cook up big meals and feed the other members. Some members will be happy to do the grocery shopping (beforehand, so they can just veg out on the couch). Others will roll up their sleeves and do the dishes. No one will want to clean the bathrooms; so it helps to assign unpleasant tasks before you even get into the car, with the agreement that everyone will pitch in to restore the place to pristine condition on the last day. When someone disappears for a last walk along the water, you have every right to make her haul the trash bags to the dump in her car's trunk. Cleanup was part of the deal!

Consider assigning different meals to different members. Each year during the weekend of the Academy Awards, Debra Lande's mah-jongg group rents a house on the coast about two hours north of San Francisco. "We assign breakfast, lunch, or dinner to different members. Everyone buys groceries separately, saves the receipts, and on the very last day we do the financial reckoning," Debra explains. And since the group puts money into a group kitty throughout the year, the house rental is usually covered, with money left over. They have even hired a masseuse to come to the house, an excellent use of club funds!

Carol Hamlin's Bible-study group has a retreat twice a year. Last winter members headed to Ely, Minnesota, for a three-day getaway. "We focused the retreat around a bit of storytelling and talking about who we are as women," Carol says. "Some women were willing to lead group discussions. They brought questions, topics, books, and articles from the Internet, which led to lively discussion. The rest of us brought food."

That sounds like a great weekend. On the other hand, a retreat can be a hotbed of tension. After all, these mini vacations generally involve the most concentrated and longest period of time your group has ever spent en masse. Personality traits that may have been hidden, tamped down, or otherwise not on display during meetings might come to the fore during a weekend away. Someone's obsessive-compulsive disorder might be revealed by the way she keeps reorganizing her (and everyone else's) drawers. Another's penchant for mischief might get the group into trouble when neighboring guests call to complain about the strange noises emanating from your suite.

Carol Hamlin's Bible-study retreats are not always heavenly. A real hullabaloo occurred in her group during an in-town retreat at a local hotel. This time, Carol was part of the problem. "We all left our husbands and young kids and bailed to a hotel for the weekend. Two of us were bored, so we went to bar and got drunk. That did not go over well. We sat at the bar and talked to men, and didn't roll into the room until 3:00 A.M. The next day the rest of the group had an intervention with us. They 'encouraged' us not to attend any more." While the other woman did indeed drop out of the group, Carol just kept showing up at the meetings. "Eventually, it all blew over. But I was stunned at the ferocious nature of their anger. It was as though I had betrayed a norm that had never come up as a norm. Before then, we tried to come on time, we stayed two hours, we rotated turns on the Bible study." Don't assume that just because you are on a retreat, which by its very nature may seem like it should be a total withdrawal from your normal existence, you can shirk your responsibilities to the group—or that the group dynamic will suddenly become laissez-faire. Consideration should still rule the day.

HOLIDAY PARTIES

In addition to arranging retreats, many groups gather to celebrate the holidays, regardless of faith. Debra Lande's San Francisco mah-jongg club has a Hanukkah party. The hostess makes latkes, and the other members bring accompaniments. The group lights candles and has a grab bag of gifts (which can't cost more than ten dollars). Artist e Bond's Art Night group gathers with food and champagne for a holiday brunch at a member's house. "We give rounds of gifts," e says. "One has to be made, one has to be regifted, and one has to cost one dollar . . . One 'gift' is an ugly metal Christmas tree that always gets regifted." For Art Night, making one of the presents is a great way to keep the theme of the group alive during the party.

What could your group do to celebrate the season while retaining the group's flavor? Your cycling club, for example, could take a holiday ride through an area of town resplendent with holiday lights and decorations before meeting at a member's house or a restaurant for dinner. Your movie club could screen a classic holiday film (*It's a Wonderful Life, A Christmas Story*) and exchange DVDs. Or your group could always choose to alter its raison d'être for the night and just get together for female fellowship and homemade eggnog.

GUEST SPEAKERS

As far as guest speakers go, advise all members to be prompt and respectful of your guest. Accommodate the guest's requests (Diet Coke in a can, for instance) to the best of your ability and, just like you would on field trips, have on hand an "emergency" supply of snacks, beverages, and pain relievers. Ask one member to research and introduce the guest, and another to create a list of discussion questions for use during a Q&A session.

Assume nothing when it comes to your guest. Ask if she would like you to arrange transportation or if she requires directions to the meeting, even if she lives nearby. Inquire whether he has any special needs regarding food, beverages, lighting, supplies, or seating. If you are asking the guest to illustrate to the group a new technique, recipe, or pattern, photocopy handouts in advance and e-mail members a materials/ingredients list so they know what to bring to the meeting. Your guest will definitely appreciate your professionalism and thoughtfulness. If your guest has a positive experience, chances are he or she will give another prospective guest a glowing review of your organization down the road.

Finding Guest Speakers

Experts are all around you. Well, maybe not in your living room, but they are close at hand. Just open your eyes a bit and put the word out. Your neighbor might be an investment banker who knows the perfect person to talk to your finance club about mutual funds. The barista at your favorite coffee shop might also work for a fabulous pastry chef who would be delighted to show your gourmet club how to make ganache. And your coworker might be an avid movie buff with an extensive collection of B movies on DVD. Chances are he'd *love* to be surrounded by women talking about the merits of various Russ Meyers movies.

Aside from putting the word out to your immediate circle, there are other ways to find guest speakers. Local colleges and universities are chock-full of experts of every kind. You could call the specific department you're interested in, the career counseling office, or the administration office for direction. Alternatively, the university operator is generally a wealth of information who can direct you to the appropriate office. You could visit the campus and put up a notice on a departmental bulletin board; some PhD candidate might love to talk about his or her dissertation topic for an hour . . . or two . . . or three . . .

Other options are to place an ad in a local daily or weekly newspaper, or to post notices in nearby businesses such as coffee shops, sporting goods stores, or grocery stores. Use other established organizations to your advantage. Often, they are comprised of helpful folks who might be inclined to give you some leads on guest speakers. They'll be even more agreeable if you offer to trade services or to participate in joint events.

Speaker Fees

Once in a while, a guest might inquire about a fee. That's unfortunate but to be expected. Review your coffers and assess whether your group can afford a modest honorarium. Even a hundred dollars goes a long way toward making a guest feel valued. If nothing else, you should offer to pay the guest's expenses. And outline the offer before he or she is left wondering and is forced to ask. When you first approach someone about speaking to the group, be up front about what you plan on paying for: a speaker's fee, travel arrangements, dinner, and so forth. Put it in writing so there is no miscommunication. This will help speed the speaker's decision and will avoid a last-minute request for a hefty fee your club just can't swing.

What Kind of Speaker Is Appropriate for Your Club?

Anything and anyone of interest to the group, however loosely connected, is a great choice for a talk. Your sailing-club members might be interested in listening to a local documentary filmmaker discuss the challenges of filming underwater—even though the subject is not immediately related to sailing. Be on the lookout for anybody who would delight or educate your members. And don't forget about your many friends. They can be highly accomplished in their respective fields and can make interesting and accommodating—not to mention free!—guests.

Here are some club-specific ideas for guest speakers:

- *Financial Club:* accountant, banker, investor, economics professor, finance writer

- *Book Club:* agent, author, editor, historian, librarian, bookstore manager

- *Culture Club:* actor, dancer, film critic, movie director, mosaic artist, painter, photographer, poet, theater set designer

- *Career Club:* CEO, headhunter, human resources attorney, human resources manager, life coach, small-business owner, Myers-Briggs administrator

- *Gaming Group:* card dealer, croupier, professional gambler, mathematician, body-language expert

- *Craft Circle:* craft-shop owner, designer, patternmaker, specialist in a particular technique, women's studies professor

- *Interest Club:* (depends on the type of group) chef, vintner, seasoned traveler, travel writer, historian, biologist, ornithologist, boat captain, pilot

- *Sporting Club:* professional athlete, personal trainer, martial artist, sports reporter, nutritionist, physical therapist, podiatrist

- *Activist or Emotional Support Group:* lobbyist, politician, publicist, doctor, minister, scientist, therapist

- *Spiritual Gathering*: meditation instructor, psychic, theology or history professor, volunteer coordinator

- *Spa Party:* aromatherapist, esthetician, herbalist, massage therapist, nutritionist, spa owner, yogi

MIX IT UP

You may just want to mix things up a little, so if it's your turn to host the meeting, start it off with a fun activity. A few hands of rummy, a trivia game, or a series of yoga sun salutations are great ways to energize your group members and remind them that they are in the club for personal growth, friendship, and sheer fun.

Here are some more ideas for a good time:

Truth or Dare: The classic slumber-party game is not just for kids. Just ask members to keep the questions clean during the truth portion of the game, and to come up with dares to challenge a quality that a particular member needs to work on, be it confidence, schedule management, or cooking ("I dare you to bring something to the next meeting that you actually made!").

Q&A: Write down questions on slips of paper and fill a bowl with them. Ask each member to pick a question and answer it. Questions could be about personal history ("What was your favorite family vacation?" or "What was your prom experience like?"), dreams ("If you could have anyone else's life, whose would it be and why?" or "What would you do if you won the lottery?"), or about the group itself ("What's your favorite part of belonging to the group?").

Spin the Bottle: Don't worry, you don't have to kiss a member of your group. Instead, sincerely compliment her about something.

Club Jeopardy: See how well everyone really knows each other. Put together a game that includes questions about various members of the group.

Quiz Show: Hand out crosswords or quizzes to get the juices flowing at the beginning of the meeting.

Charades: Not only is this a fun, team-building activity, it gets the blood pumping, which will, in turn, keep everyone awake! For a twist, pick out phrases that pertain to your group.

Conversation Starters: Throw out a few questions to begin with. Topical subjects and "what if" questions or scenarios are great ways to spark a discussion and get to know members in a new way.

The important thing is to do something unexpected or unconventional to keep the club fresh and the members energized. For instance, instead of gathering for your weekly Scrabble night, meet as a one-time-only book club instead; members can prepare by reading *Word Freak: Heartbreak, Triumph, Genius, and Obsession in the World of Competitive Scrabble Players,* by Stefan Fatsis.

DOING GOOD

Starting a scholarship fund, mentoring program, or some other outreach venture for teens or for the community is a great way to keep everyone motivated. The philanthropic activity might be a no-brainer, as was the scholarship Liesa Goins and her high school friends set up in memory of a friend who died of leukemia. Or it might take a few discussions with the group to figure out which charity or public service you'd like to devote your energies to.

One year, members of the Pulpwood Queens book club read aloud to children at the Texas State Fair, festooned in their signature tiaras and leopard prints. Afterward, they went to hear LeAnn Rimes sing. "Because of our tiaras, the crowds parted and let us go all the way to the front. And you know what? We should be treated like royalty because we're readers," says founder Kathy Patrick. Pulpwood Queens' members like to promote literacy throughout their kingdom. They visit nursing homes and read to the elderly. They even started a splinter teenage chapter that meets once a month and reads to small children. Their volunteer efforts support their mission-statement goal of getting America reading.

Even small projects can have a huge impact. One of the easiest things to do is to host fund-raisers and give a scholarship to a worthy college-bound teenager. Maria Young's mothers' group provides five hundred dollars toward a scholarship for a graduating senior. In addition, they help out parish families. "We choose a family in need and get stuff for them at Christmas," Maria says. "While we wanted to give clothes and more personal items, the family can't even afford paper products, so we asked for donations from friends and family. My brother-in-law works for Hefty, and he donated a bunch of really practical supplies. And instead of waiting until December, we helped them out before the holidays." Have your group look around—is there an opportunity to assist someone right in front of you?

CHAPTER 7

Growing Pains & Gains

So your club is going swimmingly. Congratulations! Is it going too well? In other words, is the group growing by numbers that are hard to accommodate? Are your group plans and projects too ambitious for your current members to handle? Do people from different towns want to join in your fun? Growth can be a great thing if you plan for it and manage it, but an unexpected growth spurt can be uncomfortable. This chapter will guide you through the growing pains and pleasures you're bound to experience.

It may have taken a while for your group's ranks to swell but now you are ready to require more participation of your members. Active membership will sort out the well-intentioned members from the truly committed ones, thereby naturally thinning the numbers down. But maybe you want to grow your group, or at least you may be open to the idea since all the members are fabulous and bring something to the party. With increased membership, however, come new needs, such as a larger meeting venue, greater organization, and perhaps a more sophisticated Web site or newsletter. Heck, you may even want to trademark your name or brand your club—or even consider franchising it, so that the gospel of your group can spread far and wide. How do you do this so your members, old and new, can continue to feel connected to and excited by your organization? Wow, there's a lot on your plate, so it's best to dive into this very exciting stage in the life of your group.

If you don't want to turn anyone away, you'll have to be willing to deal with the challenges of an increasingly larger club. "I'm not an event planner. All I want to do is plan *lunch*," Zoe Alexander says of the challenge of hosting monthly luncheons for Divas Who Dine. However, because the ranks swelled so quickly, she was suddenly forced to get familiar with the ins and outs of event planning, not to mention other aspects of running a business. "One of my friends is a publicist. She came to me and told me how to grow the group and be a company. We became an LLC [Limited Liability Corporation] and are in the process of trademarking our name." For the original New York group, she splits the lunches over two days (more on that later). Meanwhile, she has also started chapters in Miami, Las Vegas, and Los Angeles. Not bad for the club's first year! What could you do if you put your mind to it?

GETTING STRICT

If your group is growing or otherwise getting out of control, you'll need to rein it in with some structure and some serious adherence to that structure.

Being selective about who you invite into your group may not have been necessary at first, but if your group has grown to the point that meetings have become unwieldy, it may be time to create formal criteria for admission. Make a prospective member really work for membership.

Applications and Interviews

If you decide to implement rules and qualifications for admission, your group must first agree to always abide by them, no matter how much or how little you or another member like a prospective member. It doesn't matter if she's your sister-in-law. Play fair so that no one grumbles next week or next year that someone plays favorites.

So what should be required for admission? Depending on your group, you may want to interview a potential member or ask her to attend one meeting on a trial basis. That way, you can get a sense of how well she would mesh with the other women. If you interview her, have a few standard questions on hand, and take notes. Ask her about her background, her motivations for joining the group, her availability, her job, her preferences for working alone or in teams, and any questions specific to your group. If you are a hiking group, ask her where she's hiked and what her favorite trails are. If you are an investment club, ask her a few questions to ascertain how much or how little she knows about finance.

You may also choose to ask prospective members to fill out an application. Aside from requiring name, address, and other perfunctory information, include a few open-ended questions about background, motivation, interests, areas of expertise, and the like. It's helpful to know not only about a potential member's personality, but also if she was a CPA in a former life. And if your club pays yearly dues, ask that they be paid upon acceptance into the group. Since it takes time to process and evaluate an application, it's entirely acceptable to charge a small application fee. This will also ferret out the avid from the apathetic.

Essays are another effective way to separate the wheat from the chaff. Don't make them too demanding or esoteric. The essay should have a point—aside from demonstrating commitment and command of the English language—such as illuminating a prospective member's motivations or revealing early formative experiences. Here are a few concrete examples of essay topics:

- Describe your most lasting accomplishment.
- Recount a time when you played well with others.
- Talk about the most important person in your life.
- Describe your favorite way to cut loose.
- Explain what you are most proud of.
- Comment on a time when you didn't agree or get along with one or more women. How did you resolve the situation?

You could also ask a potential member to pitch in during one of your community service or fund-raising projects. See how game she is to help out. Depending on the focus of your club and the extent to which you want to control the membership ranks, use the application process as a means of being discriminating regarding potential members. Customize the application to the needs of your group, and tweak the process as your club matures.

But do keep in mind the nature of your group. A support group, for instance, is probably not the place for a rigorous admission policy. Sherry Petrie of Mocha Moms L.A. is against having a screening process: "I want people to come in and feel comfortable. Once you start talking to someone, you see where she's coming from. It's wonderful when you meet

Sample Application

Today's date:
Name:
Nickname (or name you prefer to go by):
E-mail address: Home phone:
                                         Work phone:
                                         Mobile phone:

Address:
Employer:
Date of birth:

What are your hobbies?

What are your skills/strengths?

Why do you want to join this group?

What do you hope to get out of membership?

Do you feel confident that you could attend meetings regularly?

Do you work better _____ solo _____ in groups?

Please provide three character references.
Name:
Relationship to you:
Phone:

Name:
Relationship to you:
Phone:

Name:
Relationship to you:
Phone:

Feel free to attach a résumé or any other material you think relevant.

someone new and hit it off with her. During initial phone calls, I kind of get a feel for who a mommy is and what she's looking to get out of this." When new moms want to join Mocha Moms L.A., filling out an application, paying nominal dues, and having an informal chat is all that's necessary.

Membership Requirements

Once a woman passes muster, don't let the work stop there. With a well-established and large group, it's very easy for members to slack off and miss more than the occasional meeting. Hey, someone else will take care of it, right? Wrong! Require members to fulfill certain duties or responsibilities in the course of a year in order to maintain membership in your group. Following are some suggested duties:

- bringing one idea or suggestion to every meeting
- driving one or more members to a meeting
- hosting one meeting or group event
- researching a topic and delivering a presentation
- arranging a field trip, guest speaker, or special event
- chairing a committee or heading a project
- recruiting one or several members
- promoting the club in the community
- volunteering with the group's favorite charity

Membership has its privileges, but it also has its responsibilities. During one meeting, do a mass sign-up or delegate a year's worth of important duties in one fell swoop. No one will complain of being given short notice or of having more work than other members if jobs are meted out simultaneously. Active membership will sort out the well-meaning but remiss members from the truly dedicated ones.

In some instances you won't need to worry too much about your ranks getting out of hand. For the Pulpwood Queens' Kathy Patrick, having hundreds of members in her original chapter doesn't present a problem, "The membership number kind of weeds itself out. People move away, people join. We've had as many as 225 women come to one meeting. No one talks at same time. We start discussing the book, then break up into four or five smaller groups, and finally come back together as a whole. The group is always fresh and new. The majority of members are in their forties to fifties, but we have members ranging from high school age to ninety." Two hundred–plus people in one space sounds challenging, but a little creativity can go a long way if you follow the Pulpwood Queens' philosophies of "the more the merrier" and "make it work." Put groups of people in different rooms. Send some to the patio or backyard. Have some head to another member's house or a coffee shop. It may not be ideal, but members are motivated and usually willing to roll with the punches for the sake of amazing support and fellowship.

EVENT PLANNING

Even if you never pictured yourself being a party coordinator, if your group meets at a restaurant or bar (because you set it up that way or because the group has grown beyond everyone's living rooms), you may find yourself improvising the role.

The Divas Who Dine, today a group of high-powered New Yorkers who meet for a monthly lunch, was started by Zoe Alexander. "The group started out informally when I set up lunch with a few women who I wanted to have lunch with. I needed to consolidate the meetings, so there were six of us. There were real ladies who lunch at the table next to us. They were nurturing and sweet and curious so we started calling ourselves 'Divas Who Dine' as a play on 'Ladies Who Lunch.'"

Growing pains soon followed.

When word leaked out, Zoe's friends were a little put out that they weren't invited to the lunch. Within days, there were thirty-five women signed on for the next luncheon. It became a production that involved finding a space, picking a menu, getting the price right, dealing with staff. "We kept getting shushed at the restaurant, so we had to get a private room," Zoe says. And that meant that Zoe had to learn all about the world of event planning.

The main activity for the group, the monthly lunch, has its challenges. In order to keep the group to a size where the women can really connect with one another, the luncheon has been divided into two dates with different speakers. Members can then choose which luncheon is more convenient or which topic sounds more interesting to them. The luncheons are held in private rooms, and the prix fixe menu consists of three courses. Each member chooses from a select menu, pays in cash, and can get a receipt in case she is able to expense the meeting.

Sounds like a piece of cake, right? Well, it took a lot of work to get things that streamlined — let alone to know which cake to order. So take a few pointers from some extremely savvy women who have worked out their own club kinks.

The Menu

When you schedule an event at a restaurant, ask for a prix fixe menu. Basically, what this means is that each woman pays the same amount for a menu that offers several appetizer, entrée, and dessert options. Zoe Alexander sets up Divas Who Dine lunches with various restaurants around Manhattan. The luncheon is always twenty-five dollars per member, includes soft drinks and coffee or tea, and consists of three courses (appetizer, entrée, dessert). Restaurants generally know to include a vegetarian option for the first two courses, but it doesn't hurt to request this up front (along with any other dietary requests such as kosher foods or nut-free dishes). Divas Who Dine member Jennifer Ashare also suggests asking for dishes that can be served family style. "Instead of having everything plated, the restaurant can put out salad, pizza, or fried calamari on the table. You can be creative with that anywhere," Jennifer adds.

Zoe Alexander also makes sure that the gratuity and tax are included in the price per head — otherwise she'd be tacking on another 20 percent and asking members to pony up extra cash or footing the extra amount herself. Neither option is very appealing, so checking on extra expenses pays off in the long run.

On the topic of beverages, depending on your club and the time of gathering, you might be tempted to factor alcohol into the prix fixe. If some members drink freely and others never indulge, this could be a loaded issue. The nondrinkers could feel resentful that they are footing the bill for the more liberal imbibers. In this case, it may be best for the members who want to drink to order their own beverages on their own tabs. If it's a midday meeting, you probably don't want your members returning to their offices half in the bag. And you certainly don't want them driving if they've been drinking. However, if you belong to a restaurant or wine club, drinking is a significant element of the gathering. Ask the restaurant if you can bring in your own alcohol, even if they charge a modest cork fee.

Negotiating the Price

Don't be shy about asking for a price break. Tell the restaurant what your budget is, up front. If they want your business—and they do—they'll find a way to make it work. If you don't give them an idea of your budget, the estimate will be higher. If they protest about your budget, it doesn't hurt to provide examples of other restaurants that have accommodated your group. You can also agree to use their facility for future meetings, say for the next two consecutive months. This will be especially appealing if the restaurant experiences slow periods. For example, December is usually busy for most restaurants and bars, with holiday office parties and increased socializing and dining out, but January and February are considerably slower. If you agree to hold your meeting at the one restaurant for all three months, the management will probably be happy to have the guaranteed business and will be more likely to cut you a deal.

Consider the type of restaurant you are approaching, and make it work to your advantage. For example, sushi and salad places do most of their business in warmer months, so book an event during the coldest month of the year to hit your target budget. Conversely, look to get a reasonable price by holding your July meeting at a fondue restaurant or a steak house.

If a restaurant offers you a wide array of selections for your prix fixe, choose simple fare like sandwiches, salads, and soups—which are satisfying, filling, easy to eat, and universally liked, and which won't put your members in a carb coma. For dessert, Divas Who Dine members often select petit fours and chocolates, which are good for sharing (or taking back to the office for a midafternoon snack). They go down easy with coffee, and members don't feel like they've overindulged with a full-on dessert.

Learn from the savvy of the Divas Who Dine when it comes to restaurant bookings. Member Jennifer Ashare, a special events director for a number of restaurants, encourages groups to talk to the local press, promoting the group and its chosen restaurant. "Partner with one restaurant and make sure it's mentioned in any news or promotional items about your group," she advises. It's a win-win situation: the restaurant gets guaranteed business from your group, and you in turn get a price break for bringing in your members and talking up the establishment all over town.

The Space

Zoe Alexander has also learned from experience that a private room is more pleasant—for the group, the restaurant, and other diners. "If you have a group under ten, you don't really need it, but a private room is always best if you can get it. Members can't get up and make speeches as easily [without it]. It's one thing to give a speech in an enclosed area but [it's] nerve-racking in front of the entire restaurant. And, of course, you don't want to disturb other diners," Zoe advises.

Also consider the kind of table groupings that will work best for your club. Divas Who Dine members had their first few lunches at a long, boardroom-like table. But they didn't get enough personal attention and had to yell to converse with women at the other end of the table. Round tables that seat eight or ten women turned out to be a much better option. Members could get conversations started more readily and were able to get to know one another better. Since people tend to float from table to table between courses, this arrangement offers ample opportunity to chat with other women who don't happen to be at your table. You could also enforce more mingling by making members change tables every course. This is particularly smart if you have guests attending (say husbands or significant others, at the Christmas party). They'll have little chance to feel bored or unwelcome.

A few other ideas for your restaurant meeting: If your club is rather large or is rapidly growing, start your session with introductions or updates on members' lives; have half the room do their introductions at the beginning of the meeting. Encourage members to keep their comments brief. (Even with this admonition, the members who go first will be likely to drone on. Don't be afraid to remind them to keep their comments short so that everyone will have a chance to speak.) Take a break while waiters take orders and members talk among themselves. After the first course or halfway through the event, resume the introductions. (Break for the guest speaker, if there is one.) This is a terrific way of spreading the conversation and presentations throughout the day, rather than sapping everyone's energy at the beginning or waiting until the end, when members are itching to leave or are just plum wore-out.

Scheduling and Booking

While there are always those women who can pull off a huge event in a couple of days, the stress involved with such an undertaking is not worth it. So don't feel the need to prove that you're Wonder Woman (we already know you are); instead, embrace your inner Franklin Planner and schedule meetings and events down to the last minute and detail.

If your group is comprised of busy women—and let's face it, it is—consider scheduling events six months in advance. Everyone will get the meeting on their calendar, and you'll have ample time for event planning.

Several groups recommend planning an event at least a month in advance—two weeks minimum if the event is local. When booking a place, you will most likely be required to give a down payment to secure the reservation. Give your members a clear deadline by which they need to RSVP and/or pay the event fee. You'll have to guarantee a number to the restaurant, and you don't want the club to have to absorb the cost of no-shows. Collect RSVPs in writing (e-mail is fine—you just need a paper trail) and payment in advance.

When negotiating with the venue, ask if they allow sponsors (who will supply or foot the bill for the drinks, food, decorations, or the like) or if they will let you provide your own alcohol. You can save a significant amount on spirits if you supply them yourself. The restaurant might agree to this and may charge a small "cork fee" for every bottle.

But monitor yourself when asking for cut rates, discounts, or special accommodations. You should have a sense of when you've asked for too much; try to discern if the booking manager is irritated or frustrated. Impress upon the manager the size of your group or the repeated business, but choose your battles and be prepared to back off now and again. Think about the influence of the women in your group. When Jennifer Ashare is booking events for different groups, she assesses the members. "Who are these people?" she asks. "Most likely, we want them to come to our restaurant. Even [those in] women's groups comprised of nonworking people have husbands or mothers or friends who can tell people about the restaurant. If you can sell who your group is and how it's going to give you residual business, you can usually negotiate." As Jennifer points out, restaurants don't usually make money off one isolated event. Booking events during slow times, getting repeat individual or group business, or booking larger events down the road is what will be appealing to the restaurant. Jennifer also suggests approaching a place that has more than one location (ideally, a restaurant chain or restaurant group). If one location is booked, the company can spread your business to another place, again making it a win-win situation.

When arranging a meeting or event at an outside venue, here are a few questions to ask that will make you appear thorough, not thoroughly exasperating:

- Are private rooms available? How many people can a room accommodate?
- Can people get separate checks? Can you factor in the gratuity?
- Are there slower times or slower days of the week that are better for scheduling an event?

Divas Who Dine member Jennifer Ashare suggests holding breakfast meetings. "They are great, and even a restaurant that's not open for breakfast can do something if the money's there." Or, if you can't gather your girls in the morning, try ending your event early in the evening so the restaurant has time to reset your space.

- Can we get a discount for delivering a sizable group or for booking the venue for several meetings?
- Which beverages are offered with a fixed price? Can we order drinks separately? Can we bring in our own alcohol? Decorations? Music?

Keep in mind that there is more than just money afoot when asking for this kind of favor. "We discourage bringing your own alcohol or even bringing in your own birthday cake," Jennifer Ashare says of the restaurant group she works for. "Reputable places are concerned with perception. We have our own pastry chef. We have an amazing wine list, even a mixologist on hand who creates new drinks. We don't want people to think that the cake you're eating is what we made or that it's our wine you are drinking. We want our staff to be showcased, and we have to keep up our own quality control." Decorations are another touchy subject for restaurants and clubs. Tasteful party favors are usually fine, but decorating the space or your tables on a main floor is discouraged. If you are meeting in a private room, the restaurant is usually more accommodating of your club's decorations.

- Can we request certain waitstaff?
- Do you supply A/V equipment? Are electrical outlets readily available?

Visit the restaurant well before your event and case the joint. Talk with staff about how you want to set up the space. Be up front with your needs and plans; no restaurant will take kindly to you sneaking in a sound system and blowing a fuse!

And here are some questions to ask *yourself* during the event-planning process:

- How far in advance should you schedule an event? How do you get members to commit, so you can ensure a certain number of people?
- How long will it take your club to plan the event and pick a venue?
- Will you want one long table or several round "8- or 10-tops"?
- Should your group switch seating after each course to encourage mingling?
- Do you need any audio-visual equipment such as a microphone or a projector and screen for your laptop PowerPoint presentation?
- Is a seating chart necessary? Do you want the tables organized around a podium or presentation area?

Jennifer Ashare offers some final sage advice to groups looking to host events at restaurants, clubs, or other establishments. "Restaurants will have done this before. Listen to them talk about what does and doesn't work. This isn't your wedding. It doesn't have to go exactly as planned. Next time, you can make it better. Work with the venue and create a partnership," she suggests. And she adds that asking someone at the venue to join your club is another very wise move. After all, Jennifer herself is now a Diva Who Dines!

BUILDING A WEB SITE

If you are open to an increased membership, or your group has grown beyond an effective e-mail or phone-tree system, it might be time to build a Web site. Don't freak! There are many ways to create modest sites to serve the basic needs of your organization. You can start with a simple home page and build from there, or you can develop a full-blown site with the help of a knowledgeable member or tech-savvy friend.

The first thing to do is to register a domain name. Go to a site such as www.networksolutions.com and type in your ideal Web site name (the closer the name is to the name of your club, the easier the Web site will be to find). If your first choice is already taken, try a variation, such as adding your hometown to the name (for instance, "knitwitsdallas.com"). Once you've settled on an available name, register with a reputable company (such as Network Solutions or even Yahoo!). Using simple search terms like "registering domain name" on Yahoo! yields several reputable companies. You can secure the name for one year or for several years. If your club is on firm ground and you're confident it will be around for a while, it's financially advantageous to register the domain name for as long as possible.

Now that you've got the name, you need a hosting site, a company that will store your site on its server and make it available to the World Wide Web. Again, there are innumerable services on the Internet that can house your Web site, so it's probably a good idea to ask some friends or even your company for recommendations.

Be sure to include the following basic items on your Web site:

- a welcome message
- your contact information
- membership requirements
- your mission statement and other key information about your club

- a schedule of meetings and events, with short descriptions of special occasions
- photos of past functions
- details of any philanthropic or volunteer projects
- advertisements (You might be able to get a discount at a restaurant if you offer to promote it on your site.)

Classes are widely available in Web site design and construction. Check the extension courses at your local college or university and pay for one willing member to take the class and become your Webmaster. Before she gets under way, however, pin down the details of the site. She will quickly become frustrated if the project is designed by a committee or continues to be tweaked and evaluated after she's already put substantial time and effort into it. Treat her as you would an outside contractor and give her as much information and feedback as possible during the site's infancy stage.

If no one in your club wants the responsibility, you can hire an outside Webmaster to build your site. Maybe one of your members has a spouse or friend who could handle the project. If you do hire a professional, the fee will depend on the number of "pages" you want to include and the time involved. Write up a short proposal outlining the scope of the project—be as detailed as possible—and send it out for bids. The more specific you can be with your design requests from the get-go, and the more finished and complete your text is from the start, the better and cheaper the result will be.

The Web designer will need to know the following:

- How many "pages" or sections do you need?
- These would include sections like Home, About Us, Contact Us, Calendar of Events, Our Members, that sort of thing.
- Will you supply edited copy electronically (on a disk or by e-mail)?
- Try to provide the designer with a sample of the text up front if possible.
- Will you provide coded text (i.e., text formatted in HTML)?
- What image is your club trying to convey?
- What kind of typeface, colors, graphics (illustrations, black-and-white

photos, clip art, and the like), and design style (business slick, fifties retro, down-home comfort, and so on) would you like to use?

- How will you supply art (digital photos, hard copies that need to be scanned)?
- Do you want sound effects or moving animation?
- Will you allow your members to post items on the site?

Divas Who Dine members take great advantage of this service, a perk that comes with membership. When one Diva, an event planner, needed invitations printed in three days, another Diva had a contact who was cheaper than other quotes and who was willing to do the work as a rush job. Whether members are apartment hunting or looking to fill gift bags, the Web site's postings are a great help.

- How often you will want to update the site (announcements, calendar, photos)?
- Will you want the designer to maintain the site, or will the group take over Webmaster duties?

Check out the Resources section for information on various clubs' Web sites; they are sure to provide inspiration for your own site.

MAINTAINING A CONSISTENT IMAGE

Make sure any promotional materials maintain a consistent look, an image that reflects the spirit of your group. If you are part of a serious investment club, you might be giving off the wrong impression if your site features animated caricatures of farm animals. Don't let one member's personal aesthetic interfere with the image of the club.

So first of all, determine what kind of feel you want your Web site and any printed materials to have. If you are a quilting-bee group, you may love all things country and homespun. If you are a hiking club, however, you may be earthy and no-nonsense. Whatever your group and member preferences, think about the image you want to present to the public before going hog wild. Divas Who Dine founder and president Zoe Alexander recommends "keeping the design simple and to the point. Our

Web site is pink—it's a girl thing. I like pink; and yellow [a contrasting color on the site] looks good with pink."

A logo, or a recognizable design created to represent the group, can be used on letterhead, newsletters, business cards, and a Web site, and will go a long way to "branding" your organization. For the quilting bee mentioned above, choose a standout sampler that can be modified and traced to become line art for your club's logo. For the hiking club, use minimal graphics and develop a streamlined logo that only uses a display typeface. Whatever the gist of your group, keep your logo clean so that it can be easily read and understood.

Once your logo is designed, give a moment's thought to a signature color. Pink is always a popular, cheerful choice, but there are other great attention-getting hues to claim for your club. Warm colors like reds and oranges are stimulating; red has traditionally been thought to be a power color. Consider warm colors for a career organization, a poker group, or even a cooking club (to stimulate the appetite). Cool tones like blues and greens are soothing, which might be appropriate for an outdoors club or meditation circle.

Regarding font and other graphics: Consistency is key, or it should be. Don't go crazy with different typefaces for headlines, body copy, captions, and the like. This becomes distracting and looks unprofessional. As a general rule, select a clean sans serif (a typeface that has no small lines—serifs—at the ends of the letters' main strokes, such as Helvetica) for headlines, and a serif face (a font that has fine lines at the ends of the characters' strokes, such as Times Roman or Garamond) for the body copy (or vice versa), and stick to them. Resist the urge to radically alter the point size for headlines and the like. Remember, consistency is professional, not boring.

Speaking of consistency, be sure your photos, illustrations, and design are up to snuff. If possible, buy a digital camera for the club that can be used to take photos of members and events. It will then be a piece of cake to upload them onto your Web site. Edit before putting all seventy-six pics from your holiday party on your site. They'll eat up room, and frankly, many of them may not be of publishable quality. The same goes for artwork. Your Web site shouldn't be a forum for your creative members to post their latest works—unless, of course, you belong to an art group, in which case your Web site is a fine venue for showcasing members' creations. (Art groups can also include a Member's Gallery on the site, where members' works can be featured without impinging on the rest of the site.) Overall, take care to monitor yourself. Don't post a photo of your new grandchild, unless you're willing to let others follow suit. Instead, e-mail the photo to your group.

Once your image is established, you will want to further cement your group's brand identity. Transfer your logo to letterhead. (You can create a template in your word processing program and distribute it to members for their use). While you're at it, don't forget business cards, which you can have printed cheaply at a local printer or online. (You can upload your card design; online printers such as www.vistaprint.com will produce professional-quality cards on a heavy card stock.)

PUBLISHING A NEWSLETTER

Sending out regular communications, whether via an electronic or a printed newsletter, is a great way to keep everyone informed and enthused.

Others are bound to see your bulletin, and it can be a powerful tool for recruiting new members—so take it seriously. Make sure someone who can write, edit, and use a spelling checker is helming it. Consider designating a newsletter or communications committee so that more than one pair of eyes will look over the text, and writing responsibilities will be spread around. Stress that deadlines are firm, since newsletters contain timely information that members will need to note in their planners. The club president should check in about a week before the mailing to make sure things are on schedule.

A good basic format is a four-page newsletter (fold an 11 x 17 inch sheet into four 8½ x 11 inch pages) that can be folded twice so as to be the size of a number 10 envelope. You can then pop the newsletter into an envelope or, more efficiently, secure the newsletter with a self-adhesive wafer seal on the edge (staples will catch on high-speed postal-processing equipment), add an address label and postage, and mail it. Check the U.S. Postal Service Web site (www.usps.com) for more mailing guidelines.

Now, how should you design your newsletter? Well, there are lots of desktop software applications you can use, such as QuarkXPress,

InDesign, and PageMaker, but even in Microsoft Word, creating a two-or three-column newsletter is possible. Play around with typefaces, type sizes (remembering to be consistent in the final product), margins, line spacing (also called leading), and indention. Once you find a look you like, input the text. If members e-mail you items, cut and paste the text into the newsletter document (remembering to save frequently), and edit and format the text. You can import digital photos or electronic artwork as well. When you are pleased with the final product, print out a set of pages and proofread the hard copy very carefully. Things look different outside of cyberspace, and errors are often easier to spot when you have a piece of paper in your hand.

When you've made all your corrections, print out a set of pages (label the order of pages very clearly) and take them to a copy shop to be photocopied onto 11 x 17 inch paper and folded. Provide a sample showing how you want the newsletter folded. Don't assume anything. It could end up being folded backward so that you don't have a visible mailing panel. Some copy shops are able to affix labels and postage as well, so check on that. Otherwise, you and a couple other members can finish up by addressing and mailing the newsletters.

PROMOTION

We've talked about promoting your club in the community through restaurant partners and the media, and through your Web site or newsletter. But there are other opportunities for spreading the word about your group.

The Mocha Moms' various PR efforts paid off with a segment of *Oprah*. When Sherry Petrie saw the show, she immediately chartered a chapter in Los Angeles. "I hosted a meet and greet: twelve moms showed up, and nine joined that day." In fact, Sherry Petrie was contacted for this book after I saw her getting a makeover on the Style Network's *Fashion Emergency*. Mocha Moms was mentioned in the piece, so I tracked Sherry down online through the club's Web site. Boston's Divas Uncorked wine club has been featured in *Ms., Newsweek, Heart & Soul* magazines, the *Wall Street Journal*, the *Boston Globe*, the *Boston Herald*, the *Boston Business Journal* newspapers, and in many other media outlets—and the group's Web site hypes this coverage. I first learned of them through the *Newsweek* article.

Promotion efforts don't have to be big to be effective. Maria Young's mothers' group wears badges during mass that say ASK ME ABOUT MY MOTHERS' GROUP! In addition, members strategically sit next to young mothers in church every Sunday. Use the resources at your fingertips. "With the help of the church, we put together a target group of families with young children and sent out a mass mailing," Maria says. This drive resulted in six new members joining the group. Think about what you and other club members can do individually and collectively to get the word out: posting notices at local businesses, sending out e-mails to the women in your company, sponsoring a little league team. Opportunities are everywhere, and brainstorming during a meeting will probably yield much promotion fruit.

"The Pulpwood Queens have become the largest 'meeting and discussing' book club in America! The Pulpwood Queens of East Texas kicked off Diane Sawyer and Charlie Gibson's 'Read This!' Book Club on *Good Morning America* and have now exploded to over six hundred members nationwide. They have appeared on Oprah Winfrey's Oxygen Network, been featured in numerous magazines, including *Southern Living, Texas Monthly, BOOK* magazine, *Time,* and *Newsweek* and have been featured in more newspapers than you can shake a stick at, including the *Shreveport Times,* the *Houston Chronicle,* the *Dallas Morning News,* the *New York Daily News, Variety,* and the *Los Angeles Times*!"

The above paragraph is taken verbatim from the Pulpwood Queens' Web site. Those gals know how to work it. Learn from these promotion professionals: rock your media contacts, and once you've got press and publicity, use that in your press kits and promotion efforts.

And guess what? There's no better way of promoting your group than by word of mouth. Networking is not a four-letter word. Back in the eighties, networking and using every opportunity to push yourself and your business became crass and outré. No more! Maybe it's because women have perfected the art of subtlety. Maybe it's because we are all so supportive of one another. Regardless, women can help one another every day and, seriously, in almost every way. Let's get to it!

"One of the major things to do is to talk to friends, husbands, parents, people working in the community and ask if they know anyone who has spaces," advises Jennifer Ashare of Divas Who Dine. "For instance, that's how Zoe [Alexander, the group's president and founder] found me. She asked a friend in business for contacts." Never be afraid to ask around and use who you know or who your friends know. They will help you out, because, well, you're good people.

INCORPORATION

At some point, your group may want to consider incorporation. Why? "For a group, it would be more about protection," says accountant Pete Jones. "Depending on the group, it could grow into a viable corporation that has value on its own (i.e., a resale value)." If you are planning on staying small, then it's not an issue, but who knows what the future holds for your girl group? It's a good idea to protect your name, product, and group from imitators if you ever see yourself branching out or branding your group.

For-profit corporations don't need to justify being in business for money, but nonprofit status requires proving that you are in business for charity or some other activity that is a support process versus a profitable one. Incorporation is easy and very quick. It normally takes about twenty-four to forty-eight hours to incorporate, and if you are OK with paying from $100.00 to $275.00, you can get it done by a professional group that does all of the paperwork for incorporation. If you want to do it yourself, it will take a bit of time.

Generally speaking, the steps are very similar regardless of whether you're interested in incorporating a for-profit or not-for-profit corporation.

You'll need to have a unique name. Normally, when an individual is incorporating oneself, one's personal name is fine. But if you want to use a name other than your actual name, come up with about three different options since the first one will probably be taken. The name has to end in a tag identifying it as a corporation, such as Inc. or Corp.

Once you have worked up the names, the state in which you are going to incorporate will run a name registration check for you—or you can contact a company that will do it for you. For example, accountant Pete Jones does all of his incorporations through a company called the Incorporators Ltd. "I just call them and they check immediately if the name is good and put a forty-eight-hour hold on it for me," says Pete. "This allows me to get back to the client and make sure that they are OK with the name."

Next, file for an EIN number with the IRS. This can be done online at www.irs.gov, or you can print out an application and send it in to the IRS office listed on the form. If you are in need of the EIN immediately, do everything online and you will get your EIN right then and there. The IRS will then e-mail you a follow-up letter about the EIN number and form; you will have to print out the form, sign it, and send it in. These processes are subject to change at a moment's notice, so always check the IRS Web site or consult an accountant for the latest procedure.

Going back to the incorporating process with the state: If you are doing this yourself, you will have to file the paperwork with the state and normally wait about two weeks for everything to come back. If you do this with a company that specializes in incorporation, you will get your material (seal and all) in about two days. Filing for yourself is not that bad, it's just a pain in terms of getting all of the paperwork correct. For example, if you don't put down the correct information about your capital stock, you may end up paying additional state tax for the stock.

A final step involves deciding whether to identify yourself as a specific type of corporation (S corporation, LLC, nonprofit corporation, or other); there is additional paperwork for each type of corporation. By default you are set up as a C corporation, just like any other corporation (IBM, Microsoft, Kraft, Federal Express, and so on). You have to specify if you want to be another type of corporation. All of the additional information for each type of corporation can be found online at the IRS site. The most painful process is the one for the nonprofit corporation. There are a series of types of nonprofit corporations. You have to identify which area you fall into (unions, charities, churches, bingo groups, and so on) and print out the paperwork to justify not paying taxes, based on the type of work that you do. There are many types of nonprofit corporations; they have to file taxes, but they don't pay any taxes. Filing is just a formality for documentation purposes. For additional information on nonprofit status, go to the following Web site: www.en.wikipedia.org/wiki/Non-profit_organization.

For more information on incorporation, check out the Incorporators Ltd. (www.theincorporators.com), an online incorporation service that will walk you through the process and lay out the benefits of incorporation.

TRADEMARKING YOUR NAME

Your group might become so popular that you begin to fear copycat clubs. Securing a domain name for your Web site is a huge step toward protecting the integrity of your club, but if the group is continuing to grow, you might consider "branding" your name by trademarking your name, logo, or catchphrase.

But it's time-consuming. "Trademarking is a bit more paperwork," says accountant Pete Jones. On a positive note, you will already have completed some of the work." Once you have all of the items mentioned for incorporation, moving to the next step of trademarking is not that bad. There is an additional fee of several hundred dollars, and if you go to the trademark Web site, you can easily request a trademark status for your corporation." Check out www.4trademark.com/trademarking.html for more information on trademarks.

ADVERTISING AND SPONSORS

As your club grows and gains clout, you might want to seek out additional support in the form of advertisers and sponsors. Approach local businesses that your members patronize and companies that your members work for with a press kit about your group and an invitation to advertise on your Web site or in your newsletter. Be friendly and professional, but remind them that you are coming to them first because they've always shown such support of your organization—and that conversely, you've given them your loyalty.

Be sure to make the following points in your press kit (put that branded letterhead and those business cards to good use here):

- size of club
- influence and careers of members
- average income level of members
- rate of membership growth
- number of Web site hits per month
- venues where your group can promote the advertiser

The group Divas Who Dine has a sponsor in Laurel/Perrier champagne (work those member contacts!) and was able to secure the

Palms Hotel "Real World" suite to kick off the Divas Las Vegas. The Divas Uncorked wine club has a long list of partners; they enjoy a mutually advantageous relationship thanks to the growing clout of the Divas. In 2004 the Divas launched the Divas Uncorked Collaborative Consortium to help wineries, distributors, and retailers expand in order to reach new consumer markets, specifically women and all people of color. How's that for using their power wisely?

The Pulpwood Queens book clubs, which originated in Texas, have grown to more than six hundred members nationwide; because of the clubs' influence, publishers pay for authors to attend their meetings (other chapters phone in for the discussions). Founder Kathy Patrick saw lots of opportunities and took advantage of them all. Touting her book store/beauty salon, Kathy easily persuaded Redken to sponsor the club. "Book clubs and word of mouth are selling books these days. I have the largest 'meeting and discussing' book club in America. No one franchised them, even though there are thousands of clubs around America," Kathy says. As Kathy illustrates, you can be confident without being boastful. Speak the truth about your club's assets and you too can reel in outside support.

FRANCHISING YOUR GROUP

If you are reading this book with the aim of starting a group, it's probably impossible to imagine becoming so successful that you want to branch out. But believe it or not, some groups have grown and gone on to franchise their organizations. If your group is continuing to grow both in terms of numbers and geography, it might be time to consider franchising your business. Once you've incorporated and trademarked your club, you have laid the groundwork to take things one step further and set up chapters or branches in other areas of the country.

If you think your group is unique and that it is important for another group of women to adhere to your systems, structure, and tenets, then franchising may be for you. If you want to achieve world domination, then—again—franchising is probably a good call. Additionally, franchising is a means to achieve greater profits, if that is something your group aims to do. But while a franchising fee will indeed add money to your coffers, as might the profitable work of another chapter down the road, you will have more paperwork, supervision, and overall management on your plate.

A Web site like www.franinfo.com can help you assess whether your club is ripe for franchising and if so, how to begin. Talking to an attorney, accountant, or someone who's already gone through the franchising process will be invaluable as well.

If your group does choose to go the franchise route, it's critical that you put systems in place and that you document them religiously for all new chapters. This means detailing information on training, meeting structure, promotion, accounting, and so on. In addition, you'll need to create a document called a Uniform Franchise Offering Circular (UFOC), which should include the following:

- information on the owners and officers of the group
- a breakdown of the required investment (how much the new chapter will have to pay)
- audited financial statements for the last three years
- the franchise agreement itself
- a listing of existing franchises, if any
- litigation history, if any
- other information on the company, such as the group's mission statement, philosophy, and message

The Federal Trade Commission requires that the UFOC be given to a potential chapter at the first personal meeting, or at least ten days prior to the signing of the franchise agreement and the payment of the franchise fee.

Once the paperwork is put together and put to bed, one of your members should visit the new chapter and train the members in the ways of your group. You will need to emphasize how important it is for the new chapter to adhere to the organization's systems, philosophy, and message. To ensure that the new chapter is not pursuing their own path by instilling a unique group flavor or developing their own projects, check in regularly. Offering support, sending out e-mails and newsletters, and maintaining a constant stream of communication will help make the new chapter feel welcome into the folds of your organization, not put off by Big Brother, or in this case, Big Sister. And of course, being open to the new chapter members' suggestions and opinions will truly make this a mutually advantageous relationship.

Kathy Patrick has been quite successful with franchising the Pulpwood Queens across the country. And she's worked out the kinks so that joining up is a piece of cake and running the monthly meetings is even easier. "The majority of chapters run between ten and thirty. Everyone who joins the book club pays twenty-five dollars and receives a certificate and membership card," Kathy says. "I run three chapters and send discussion questions to the head queen of the other chapters. The chapters decide where they are going to meet and if they will have refreshments. The author of the month's selection will call in and do a teleconference with all the book clubs. We also arrange for them to visit as well—we can do teleconferences from my bookstore with other chapters." What an inspired way to keep everyone on the same page!

It's great to celebrate a new chapter, so encourage your current group to put out the welcome mat in ways both large and small. When the Divas Who Dine launched a Las Vegas chapter, the group used its contacts to have the kickoff party in the Palms Hotel & Casino's "Real World" suite. Divas from New York traveled to Las Vegas to meet the new chapter's members and make them feel welcome.

Here are a few ideas for keeping your friends close and your new chapters closer:

- Drop in on their meetings for a surprise visit. (Come bearing gifts—you don't want them to feel you are checking up on them.)
- Invite the chapters' members to your meetings.
- Pair up members from different chapters to work on intrachapter projects or just to develop friendships.
- Arrange a clubwide retreat in a location convenient to all groups.
- Host a clubwide holiday party in a festive location.
- Ask other chapters' members for their opinions.
- Send out e-mail updates and ask all chapters to do the same.
- Report chapter news on your Web site or in your newsletter.
- Ask all members to submit their biographical or professional information,

and make a database available on your Web site so you can use all member contacts to your advantage.

Acknowledge that another chapter is going to be comprised of personalities different than those in your group—and that's OK! Don't expect to see the same dynamics and decisions coming out of their group. Decide which elements of your group are unique and important to maintain. Other than that, allow the other chapter to grow and find its own way. Before long, your entire organization will be teaming with energy, ideas, and buoyant attitudes.

CHAPTER 8

The Groups

Now that you have the tools necessary to start a girls' group, here are some additional ideas and suggestions for your particular group or groups. (Why choose just one? Why not start or join several?)

Congratulations, and good luck on your adventures in female bonding, support, and growth!

FINANCIAL CLUB

Women are truly doing it for themselves, and nowhere is this more evident than in the growing number of female investment, budgeting, and finance groups. Women are coming together to pool their resources and invest in female-run publicly traded companies or other companies they believe in.

Personalities suited to this type of club: Type A+ personalities
Group vibe: Power brokers
Formality/responsibility: Rules and structure highly recommended. Members must be responsible for finances and club tasks.
Ideal size: Ten or fewer
Meeting locations: Members' homes, office conference rooms after hours or during lunch
Frequency of meetings: Monthly

Meeting/hosting ideas/themes:
■ This club could suffer from taking itself too seriously, so consider taking

fifteen minutes at the start or end of each meeting to chat with one another about non-club-related topics.

- Think green to help visualize money and wealth. Decorate in hues of emerald and Kelly green, and serve salad, spanakopita, and other green foods. Apple martinis will wash everything down with the color of money.

- *Greed Is Good:* Celebrate the financial hubris of the eighties by decorating your place according to theme and by wearing clothing Bret Easton Ellis would be proud of. Think gray pinstripe and neck bows, but also neon, leg warmers, and crazy hair and makeup. Serve up martinis, wine coolers, and white wine spritzers, and toast to Gordon Gekko and unabashed enthusiasm for money.

- *Monopoly Night:* If you've been working really hard to research and invest, take a night off and play a fierce game of Monopoly. Buy and sell real estate with strategy or abandon—and stop worrying about your real portfolio for a few hours. Serve up kids' snacks, such as Kool-Aid (yeah, you can spike it), Goldfish crackers, licorice, string cheese, and PB and J.

Pay special attention to: Adhering to a structure, finding and agreeing on stocks to invest in, setting up an account, assigning roles to members

BOOK CLUB

Book clubs are one of the most common types of girl groups out there. With only one or two girlfriends, you can put together a fantastic club and get cultured at the same time. Finally read all those classics you missed in high school, or stay on the cutting edge of contemporary fiction. It's your very own book-of-the-month club.

Personalities suited to this type of club: Chatty Cathys and bookworms
Group vibe: Respectful and engaging
Formality/responsibility: Book clubs can be pretty informal. The chief concerns are book selection, discussion protocol, and meeting location.
Ideal size: Fifteen or fewer. Many women will want to join, but beware of

growing the group to a size a living room can't accommodate, let alone a size where no one opinion can be heard over the din.

Meeting locations: Members' homes, coffee shops, local parks

Frequency of meetings: Monthly. Of course, if you are a group of busy women who are reading ambitious Thomas Pynchon novels, you might want to meet every two months.

Meeting/hosting ideas/themes:

■ *Theme-of-the-month:* Decorate based on the month's book selection. For instance, have a Southern belle–themed evening with mint juleps and blues music if you're reading a Pat Conroy or Rebecca Wells novel. Give guests mini bottles of Southern Comfort when they leave (advise them not to indulge until they are safely home).

■ *Print Shop:* Surprise your club when it's your turn to host by setting up a workshop where everyone can make handcrafted journals. Supply special handmade papers, magazine covers, book jackets, and even vintage scarves that can be glued to a cardboard backing to create a sturdy book cover. With a hole punch, create holes in your cover, and in plain white paper, string ribbon through the cover and pages, and tie. Voilà, a special journal for members to use to record their notes as they are reading the next month's selection. Just make sure you leave enough time at the start of your workshop to discuss that month's book, unless you can multitask and talk while you create. Serve drinks with a straw so members can keep their hands free.

Pay special attention to: Controlling the size of the group, selecting the books, assigning someone to lead the conversation, creating discussion points

But don't be afraid to think big. The Pulpwood Queens book club hosts an annual gathering of girl groups (including book clubs) at the convention center in Jefferson, Texas. Founder Kathy Patrick describes one of the recent get-togethers: "The whole town filled with hot pink T-shirts and tiaras. We had sixteen authors and speakers last year, and all the authors who came are telling all their friends. It's the only book festival I've seen that centers around female friendships and books."

Picking the next book to read can be a contentious matter, so even if you have a casual, small group, it pays to establish that each member takes turns picking a book. Of course, members can suggest books. Do so in advance; e-mail is a great tool. It's helpful to provide a review or a link to a Web site like www.amazon.com so members can easily check out the book's particulars. It's even advisable to pick a few months' worth of selections at once so members have ample time to read the more lengthy tomes. It's also wise to limit the selections to paperback only, in order to keep costs down. New releases are usually pricey hardcovers with long waiting lists at the library.

Some groups like to stick with material that falls into a particular category: fiction, classics, books by contemporary female authors, and so on. This certainly helps you narrow down the many choices, but you might miss out on reading and discussing that hot new biography that everyone *but* your club is talking about.

Do take into consideration the amount of discussion a genre of books will generate. Historical romances, plot-driven thrillers popular in airport bookstores, or books about uptown nannies are fun to read but often don't merit an hour-long conversation.

Tried-and-true book selections: These are just a few of my favorites from my own book club experiences. If you've read all of these, you might want to check out these authors' newer works. Some of the books even come with discussion questions or author Q&A sections, which provide nice jumping-off points for a book club—don't you think?

NOVELS

    Bastard Out of Carolina, Dorothy Allison
    The Feast of Love, Charles Baxter
    The Amazing Adventures of Kavalier & Clay, Michael Chabon
    The Crimson Petal and the White, Michel Faber
    The Autobiography of Henry VIII, Margaret George
    Bee Season, Myla Goldberg
    Stones from the River, Ursela Hegi

A Widow for One Year, John Irving

The Poisonwood Bible, Barbara Kingsolver

Atonement, Ian McEwan

The Magician's Assistant, Ann Patchett

The Lovely Bones, Alice Sebold

The Divine Secrets of the Ya-Ya Sisterhood (screen the movie adaptation at
    your meeting), Rebecca Wells

SHORT STORIES

The Girls' Guide to Hunting and Fishing, Melissa Bank

Come to Me, Amy Bloom

Cowboys Are My Weakness, Pam Houston

The Interpreter of Maladies, Jhumpa Lahiri

Anything by Alice Munro

MEMOIRS/ESSAYS

Boys of My Youth, Jo Ann Beard

All Over But the Shoutin', Rick Bragg

Dry, Augusten Burroughs

Running with Scissors, Augusten Burroughs

A Heartbreaking Work of Staggering Genius, Dave Eggers

Personal History, Katharine Graham

The Kiss, Katherine Harrison

The Liars' Club, Mary Karr

Truth & Beauty, Ann Patchett

Use Me, Elissa Schappell

Me Talk Pretty One Day, David Sedaris

Naked, David Sedaris

Take the Cannoli, Sarah Vowell

A Supposedly Fun Thing I'll Never Do Again, David Foster Wallace

NONFICTION

Blink, Malcolm Gladwell

The Tipping Point, Malcolm Gladwell

The Island of Lost Maps, Miles Harvey

The Perfect Storm, Sebastian Junger
Brunelleschi's Dome, Ross King
Into Thin Air, Jon Krakauer
Savage Beauty: The Life of Edna St. Vincent Millay, Nancy Milford
Longitude, Dava Sobel
The Professor and the Madman, Simon Winchester

CULTURE CLUB

Now that *Sex and the City* only lives on through DVD and syndication, women are turning to other cultural events or programs as reasons to gather on a weekly (or regular) basis. Movies, art, theater, music, and TV offer low-key opportunities for women to gather, soak up some culture or pop culture, and then debate the merits of the evening's entertainment.

Personalities suited to this type of club: Culture vultures
Group vibe: Cutting-edge
Formality/responsibility: Culture clubs can be formal, with dues and lots of field trips and speakers, or as informal as having a few women over every week for a movie or TV show.
Ideal size: Ten or fewer for an informal group. More for a structured group—you may be able to solicit group discounts and special speakers when you have a larger size.
Meeting locations: Members' homes, coffee shops, theaters, galleries
Frequency of meetings: Weekly (if there's a TV show you gather to watch and dissect), every two weeks, or monthly

Meeting/hosting ideas/themes:
- *Oscar Oscar!:* Gather together on the big night to watch the red carpet preshow and the awards ceremony. Invite nonmembers and—gasp!— men to the event. Perhaps you can even charge admission and rent out a local theater space (as long as you can set up a television and screen). Demand that everyone dress to the nines, whether or not they have a personal stylist and makeup artist. Create a ballot for members to fill out beforehand and turn in. Make sure to include a tiebreaker, such as "How long will the Oscar telecast be?" or "Which movie won the Best

Picture Oscar in 1939?" (make it a multiple-choice question). Give a prize (movie passes, basket of movie popcorn and candy, DVD of a nominated film) to the person with the most correct answers. Serve a fun cocktail, such as a sidecar or mojito, to enliven the crowd. And don't forget the popcorn!

- *Film Festival:* Check out your local film festival. Many cities host great independent or themed film festivals (gay and lesbian film festivals are particularly popular), so take advantage of this opportunity to see films that may never enjoy widespread distribution. Pick a double feature and buy tickets in advance. Hand out small bags of popcorn or treats (if allowed) as your members enter the theater. Easy-peasy. Alternatively, host your own film festival in your home theater. Rent two or three movies and run a movie marathon on a Saturday. Pick a theme, such as female directors (Allison Anders, Jane Campion, Sofia Coppola, Callie Khouri, and so on), foreign films (*La Femme Nikita, Nights of Cabiria, Rashomon*), Southern dramas (*The Apostle, The Prince of Tides, Steel Magnolias, To Kill a Mockingbird*), film noir (*Dial M for Murder, DOA, The Maltese Falcon, Sunset Boulevard, The Third Man*), catty chick flicks (*All about Eve, Stage Door, The Women*), disaster movies (*The Poseidon Adventure, Titanic, The Towering Inferno*).

- *Poetry Slam, Bam, Thank You Ma'am!:* Whether or not your members are born poets, ask them all to write a piece of prose or poetry to read at your next meeting. Set up a stage and a microphone (if available) and let your members release their inner Dickinson, Millay, or Rossetti. Request that only kind, supportive feedback be given.

- *Recital:* Like at the poetry slam, ask members to come prepared to perform. This time, however, ask the gals to pick a portion of their favorite play or novel. Make copies of play scenes, assign parts to different members, and conduct a "table reading." If members sing, ask them to perform a favorite song for the group. They could even lead a sing-along. Present every performer with a comedy-tragedy charm or some such token of appreciation.

- *Painting Party:* Get out colored pencils, watercolors, finger paints, or clay, and have members replicate their favorite work of art in whatever medium they choose. Take the show on the road: channel your starving art student: take sketchbooks to a gallery and draw a masterpiece. Compare your works in a "gallery exhibition" at the next meeting. Instruct everyone to wear black.

- *Passport Party:* Pick a city and present a movie or some music or art from or about the spot. Of course, feature a signature dish and drink from your exotic locale. This would be a fun theme to incorporate for an entire year. Each hostess would be in charge of that month's "trip."

Pay special attention to: organizing outings, delegating responsibility, handling money

CAREER CLUB

Especially around the age of thirty, women start questioning their career choices and may even contemplate a career switch. Consequently, groups are popping up that aid in networking and life coaching, not to mention plain old support for women wanting to take their careers to the next (or a new) level.

Personalities suited to this type of club: Divas with drive and mavens with moxie
Group vibe: This Good Young Girls' Club turns the traditional Good Old Boys' Club on its ear with energy and savvy.
Formality/responsibility: Somewhat formal, with regular meetings, group projects, individual assignments, and stated goals
Ideal size: The more the merrier, as everyone can benefit from one another's talents and networking abilities.
Meeting locations: Members' homes, office conference rooms
Frequency of meetings: Monthly

Meeting/hosting ideas/themes:
- *Good Old Girls' Night:* Why do good old boys get to kick back with aged liquor and red meat? Bust out the filet mignon, cigars, and scotch, and

have a decidedly un-PC evening telling tall tales, objectifying men, and calling in favors.

■ *Brown-bag It:* Meet for lunch in the park to discuss different career paths, educational/training opportunities, or a new topic in your field. This is an excellent venue for a guest speaker, as it's often easier to secure a guest during the workday than in the evening. Bring lots of blankets so no gal gets grass stains on her best suit.

■ *Mentor Mixer:* Post signs at colleges and high schools, and ask young women in the neighborhood to attend a meeting. During the meeting, take turns sharing your expertise with young career women, and consider pairing members with newbies on an on-going basis. Serve soft drinks and light snacks at the meeting, wear name tags, and ask members to introduce themselves to as many guests as possible. Hey, you might infuse your club with fresh blood as well!

Pay special attention to: Determining the focus of the group, arranging guest speakers

GAMING GROUP

Be it for cards, bingo, board games, or casino outings, women are coming together to unleash the serious gambler or playful competitor within. Whatever your group's focus, make sure everyone's comfortable with the stakes, and mix up the game choice once in a while. Note that many forms of gambling are illegal in various states (check out http://www.gambling-law-us.com/State-Laws/) so consider paying yearly dues and gambling for prizes instead of money, or putting the winnings toward a fabulous group retreat.

Personalities suited to this type of club: Gals with game
Group vibe: Rowdy and often competitive
Formality/responsibility: While a game face is respected, make sure your gals are on the up-and-up when it comes to playing fair.
Ideal size: It depends on the game. Board games, mah-jongg, and bridge

are best kept to a small number of players (such as four); bingo is best with a bunch. A larger group, however, can easily break into smaller groups, even rotating between hands or games.

Meeting locations: Members' homes (gambling is still illegal in most states!)

Frequency of meetings: Weekly for true addicts—uh, enthusiasts; every two weeks or monthly for others

Meeting/hosting ideas/themes:

- *Casino Royale:* Host a casino night, with friends or spouses acting as dealers. Set up tables with blackjack and poker. Rent a roulette wheel or craps table. Put on some Rat Pack tunes, offer free drinks, and send everyone home with dice or a deck of cards.

- *Game Grab Bag:* If poker's your poison, pull out the Scrabble board for a fun change of pace. If mah-jongg's your game of choice, play dominoes or backgammon instead. Print out instructions for everyone if you are learning a new game so members can study up.

- *Board-game Pajama Party:* Channel your inner child and host a slumber party, complete with favorite games from childhood. Ask members to bring comfy clothes (preferably pajamas) and spread out on the floor with Monopoly, the Game of Life, and Trivial Pursuit. Serve Kool-Aid with PB and J; for dessert make s'mores. And remember, you don't have to play poker to bet competitively.

   Pay special attention to: Differing personalities (competitive vs. social), betting, gambling styles (conservative vs. strategist vs. big spender), knowing the rules

CRAFT CIRCLE

Whether it's a new stitch 'n' bitch knitting circle or a longstanding quilting bee, craft groups are growing in number and diversity. Craft circles are great for enthusiasts of knitting, quilting, scrapbooking, beading and jewelry making, journaling, needlepoint, crochet, candle making, and the like.

Personalities suited to this type of club: Crafty ladies

Group vibe: Supportive and nurturing

Formality/responsibility: Since women are usually working on individual projects, this can a pretty loose group that gathers to chat while being creative. However, if the focus of your group is on constructing a project for charity or display, more teamwork and commitment will come into play and you'll need to be more formal, with dues, delegation, and the like.

Ideal size: Fifteen, if you have the room

Meeting locations: Members' homes, community rooms, empty classrooms or office conference rooms

Frequency of meetings: Monthly

Meeting/hosting ideas/themes:

- *Color Clinic:* Gather a host of colorful swatches from a local fabric shop and conduct a seminar on color matching and color therapy. Color wheels, available at arts and craft shops, show complementary and contrasting hues and intensities. Studying one will be very helpful no matter the focus of your craft circle. You can also distribute handouts on color theory; warm colors like red and orange are stimulating, cool tones like green and blue are soothing. Serve colorful drinks (food coloring is your friend) and ask members to wear their most vibrant togs.

- *Brainstorming Barnstormer:* Ask all women to come to a meeting with a wish list of projects they'd like to make or roadblocks they are experiencing in the creative process (one woman keeps making variations on the same theme; one always chooses a safe pattern and doesn't challenge herself; one is forever drawn to the same color palette, and so on).

- *Movie Night:* Rent something about women and creativity, such as *How to Make an American Quilt*, and revel in the wonderful circle of friends and craftswomen you belong to. Maybe you can take a break from your usual crafts and work on a group project or fun craft to take home (such as a cool Christmas ornament or mobile).

Pay special attention to: Lighting and work space, group projects, working for charity, learning new techniques, tidiness when working on projects

INTEREST CLUB

No matter how esoteric your interest—be it motorcycles, wine tasting, travel, or bird-watching—there is a club for you. There are as many different interests as there are women out there, so use the ideas here to inspire your club or give you an idea for a new one.

Personalities suited to this type of club: Obsessive—um, I mean, enthusiastic—hobbyists

Group vibe: Kindred spirits sharing the love of their hobby or passion

Formality/responsibility: The club could be as casual or rigid as you want. For instance, a biker group could just plan to go riding every Saturday morning, weather permitting, with a different member choosing the route. Or a travel club might meet once a month, do copious research, require serious dues and payment, have a formal voting structure, and have various rules when actually on trips.

Ideal size: The sky's the limit.

Meeting locations: Depends on the group—the open road, the wilderness, a member's kitchen, and so on

Frequency of meetings: Weekly, every two weeks, monthly

Meeting/hosting ideas/themes:

■ *Ask the Expert:* Members of your group might have particular expertise in one subject. Ask them to share their knowledge during one meeting or over several. They can come with handouts or props. End each talk with a Q&A session.

■ *Cinema Passionada:* No matter your group, there exists a movie that will speak to your collective passion. Dim the lights at a member's house and pop in a movie. *Easy Rider* will rev up your motorcycle club, *Sideways* will juice up your oenophiles, *Big Night* is a foodie's dream, and *The Birds* will send your bird-watching club on a flight of fancy. Don't forget the movie candy and popcorn.

- *Retreat:* Block out a weekend to spend with your group. Rent a house in the mountains or at the beach (or in wine country or a prime whale-watching coastal region . . .) and spend the weekend doing and talking about what you all love. Before the trip, make a communal shopping list for group meals, and stock up on groceries, which should be paid for with dues or reimbursed equally by members. Alternatively, ask women to just bring their own supplies and snacks. Pack some board games or cards so you can really unwind in the company of good friends.

Pay special attention to: Coming to a consensus about activities, rain dates, finances, delegating responsibilities

SPORTING CLUB

A common way for women to come together is through fitness. Myriad clubs exist for women who want to run, hike, bike, or climb mountains — and that's just for starters. Speaking of starters, different clubs have different fitness requirements. Make sure the members in your club are in the same general shape and have the same fitness goals. You don't want a woman looking for a bit of exercise to be holding up your fifty-mile cycling trip to a historic battlefield.

Personalities suited to this type of club: Jocks
Group vibe: Super-supportive and energetic, thanks to all those endorphins
Formality/responsibility: Depends. For longer mountain climbing or hiking trips, planning and fees are necessary for transportation, food, and/or lodging. Running and cycling clubs, however, can just get together on a weekly basis for runs and rides around town or the surrounding area.
Ideal size: Twenty or fewer
Meeting locations: Usually outdoors, at locations ideal for your sport: paved back roads for cyclists and runners, mountains for climbers and hikers, lakes and oceans for kayakers, streams and rivers for fly fisherwomen, and so on. Obviously, it will be a bit hard to start a sailing club if you're landlocked or a snowshoeing club if you're in Florida, so pick a club appropriate to your surroundings.
Frequency of meetings: Weekly or monthly

Meeting/hosting ideas/themes:

- *Pageant Prizes:* During one of your outings, give prizes for the most improved member ("Miss Got-her-game-on") or most supportive member ("Miss Encouragement"). You can also spring more lighthearted categories on the group, like "Miss Two-left-feet" or "Miss Snappy Patter" (for the club clown) to keep spirits high and good-humored. You could even make sashes for the winners to wear during a gathering.

- *Body Clinic:* Consider hiring a trainer or physical therapist to lead a strengthening or flexibility clinic. Hand out ice packs or Epsom salts for members to use after a particularly tough workout. Serve up heart-friendly or energy-boosting snacks for a good pick-me-up.

- *Seeing Red:* Ask members to wear a stimulating color such as red or orange to your next gathering. You'll feed off the energy and present a powerful presence to the world. Of course, bring red snacks, such as licorice, cranberry juice, and dried cherries.

- *The Safety Dance:* For one meeting, discuss safety procedures. Even if your members are aware of them, it never hurts to have a refresher course. Consider holding this once a year. Check into any new trail maps, regulations, or national park information and distribute pamphlets or handouts to members. Give out reflector patches for women to wear or put on their equipment. Check your equipment and gear together, tightening, cleaning, and repairing anything that looks shaky. Include examples of avoidable accidents as cautionary tales, and share your fears with one another.

Pay special attention to: Safety, trip planning, traveling

ACTIVIST OR EMOTIONAL SUPPORT GROUP

If your feelings and passions are running high, chances are that others are seconding that emotion. Take action or at least gather some like-minded souls together to support a cause or support one another.

Personalities suited to this type of club: Passionistas or sensitive souls

Group vibe: Intense

Formality/responsibility: While the group might not have a lot of rules, it is important that members show up consistently and don't just use the club when they need to feel better or find an channel for their outrage.

Ideal size: For the activist group, as many as possible. For the support group, a small number—fifteen or fewer—will help foster trust and intimate conversations.

Meeting locations: Members' homes, parks, community centers

Meeting/hosting ideas/themes:

- *Dream Team:* Dreams matter, so bring them out of the dark and into your group. Host a night to talk about your hopes and dreams with one another. Who knows? Maybe another member will have an idea on how to achieve that dream, no matter how far-fetched it seems. Hang stars from the ceiling, serve up mulled cider and comfort foods, and really indulge the body and spirit.

- *Playdate:* Stop taking everything so seriously and head to the playground. Take over the monkey bars and merry-go-round and play in the grass. Grill hot dogs and burgers and wash it all down with Kool-Aid.

- *Rabble Rouse:* Find a cause, event, or upcoming rally to support, and spend a meeting mapping out a strategy of support (or protest, as the case may be). Assign someone to handle the bullhorn, another to transport members or signs, and so on. And just to show your support of your club, make a few signs pledging your support. A catchy chant for the group, come to think of it, would be really fun and would get everyone fired up. As each member comes in, pin a homemade protest button on her. This evening is guaranteed to light members' fires or add further fuel to the fire!

Pay special attention to: Warring opinions, emotional instability, spreading your message outside the club

SPIRITUAL GATHERING

Women are constantly searching to bring meaning and value into their busy lives, and one way to do this is through a spiritual gathering. Bible study, meditation, Kabbalah, Wicca, Buddhism, even divination gatherings exist for women to explore the unknown, both in the universe and within themselves.

Personalities suited to this type of club: Spirituality seekers, New Agers

Group vibe: Transcendent, peaceful, and accepting

Formality/responsibility: Informal in many ways, spiritual groups can benefit from some ground rules (examples: meetings should always start with an intention; when meditation begins, no one can speak until an agreed-upon time; Bible study will explore one female-related passage or story per meeting).

Ideal size: Ten or fewer

Meeting locations: Places of worship, members' homes, local parks

Frequency of meetings: Weekly or monthly

Meeting/hosting ideas/themes:

■ *Summer Solstice:* Celebrate the longest day (and shortest night) of summer—around June 22—with a party honoring the stars. Hand out small books on astronomy or constellations, work up members' birth charts (see www.alabe.com, where it's easy and free), and celebrate the earth and the skies. Serve up the fruits and vegetables of summer, and thank the heavens for nurturing you and the bounty you are enjoying. Send members home with a small bag of summer squash, strawberries, tomatoes, or whatever's in season in your area.

■ *The Goddess Within:* Honor goddesses of legend and history with a night devoted to all things goddess. Have each member toast to her favorite goddess and then talk about her own favorite goddesslike qualities. Hand out books on mythology, or African fertility dolls as reminders to always respect the goddess within.

■ *Sing-along:* Let the spirit lift you with a night of gospel singing. While you don't have to wear choir robes, find a soundproof area to meet (a place of worship, perhaps) and encourage members to sing as loud and passionately (and perhaps badly) as they want. Supply tea with honey to soothe the vocal cords. You never know, you may find a Mahalia Jackson or Whitney Houston in your group, or you might like it so much that your club decides to begin each meeting with a hymn or rockin' gospel tune.

Pay special attention to: Controlling spiritual discussions with kindness and an open mind, selecting passages for study, keeping discussions fresh

SPA PARTY

More and more women are making products and treating one another to spa treatments on a regular basis. What's not to like? Avoid the pricey salon fees and catch up on the latest gossip with your best gal pals.

Personalities suited to this type of club: Glamour pusses
Group vibe: Relaxed and indulgent
Formality/responsibility: As informal as you can get (except for a strict "no cell phones" rule) —this group is all about chilling out.
Ideal size: ten or fewer
Meeting locations: Members' homes, local spas or gyms
Frequency of meetings: Monthly, if possible!

Meeting/hosting ideas/themes:

■ *Woo Woo Women:* Dive into all things New Age at a meeting. Perform crystal therapy on one another, have a reiki specialist treat members and talk about their energy, perform aromatherapy massages, or educate the group on chakras with some accompanying exercises to open different chakras. Make sure you have handouts so members can investigate alternative treatments on their own.

■ *Dogs Are Barking:* Indulge the unsung heroes that are your feet. Invite members to bring their dogs to play in the backyard while you give one another foot massages and spa pedicures. Make sure to paint toes a particularly shocking shade of red or burgundy or electric blue—anything but Ballet Slippers or some equally delicate shade. Make biscotti in the shape of bones and send members home with doggie and people treats to enjoy while admiring their feet.

■ *Spa Exotic:* Research different skin and beauty treatments from a particular country or region. Whether it's slathering your skin with exfoliating Kona coffee grounds or detoxifying mud, liven up your group with an exotic spa experience. Decorate with exotic sari fabric or calming Asian colors, serve Darjeeling or jasmine tea, and warm members up with some ashtanga yoga or belly dancing basics. Just do your best to focus on one region at a time, and save another cool treatment for a future spa party.

Pay special attention to: Keeping the cost within reason, gift bags, tried-and-true spa treats. It's easy for members to get carried away, either ratcheting up the "wow" factor every month or making some members uncomfortable because they can't afford to go all out. If this starts happening, suggest that everyone bring a treat (edible or topical) so everyone is contributing something at each gathering.

Congratulations on your adventures in girl groups! By now your club is probably humming along with grace and goodwill. At this point, start talking up the wondrous thing that is your women's group. Help other women find their own circle of support in which to thrive and grow. Brainstorm with them and give them tips that you had to learn the hard way. Making just one task or issue easier to handle will free that group up to focus on more important tasks, like learning how to make sushi, gambling the night away, creating a group quilt, promoting world peace, or even taking over the world. Who's to say what can be accomplished when women put their heads and hands together?

RESOURCES

RESOURCES

If you want to join a preexisting group, look on the Web for guidance, and ask women around you. Some of the clubs mentioned in this book are franchised, so contact them about starting a club in your area or joining an existing chapter.

Here's a bit more information on the amazing women and girl groups featured in the book.

DIVAS UNCORKED™

www.divasuncorked.com

"Since 1999 our ten-member group has met monthly helping each other learn about wine—from the nuances of bouquet, and the tradition of vintage, to the fusion of food-and-wine pairings. At our gatherings we travel 'via the vine'—sampling and savoring wines from around the world. We've expanded our gatherings to include special wine-centered activities, along the way fostering relationships with vintners, sommeliers, and wine educators. And, we've taken our private education public—hosting our 2004 and 2005 'Wine, Women and . . .' Conferences and Vintner Dinners since 2002."

DIVAS WHO DINE

www.divaswhodine.com

"Divas Who Dine, LLC, is a high-end social club for ladies (divas) and gentlemen (divos) in the media, fashion, food, and lifestyle industries. Similar to old-fashioned men's clubs, DWD provides a structured and supportive system of giving and receiving business, as well as pooling the group's clout together to benefit charitable organizations nationwide. It does so by providing an environment in which ladies develop personal relationships with dozens of other qualified young business professionals. DWD has proven that when DIVAS motivate, help each other and those less fortunate than ourselves—we rock!"

MOCHA MOMS

National organization: www.mochamoms.org
Los Angeles chapter: www.members.tripod.com/mommyofv-ivil/

"Mocha Moms is a support group for mothers of color who have chosen not to work full-time outside of the home in order to devote more time to their families. While many of our members have eliminated employment altogether, others work part-time, flex-time, night shifts; have home-based businesses; consult or freelance from home; or have chosen alternative, less demanding career paths so that they are more available to their families. Our goal is to support the decisions made by our members. We will never pass judgment on mothers who choose to make or are forced to make different decisions for their families. Mocha Moms welcomes people of all religions, races, educational backgrounds and income levels. Anyone who supports the mission of Mocha Moms is welcome to join."

THE PULPWOOD QUEENS
www.beautyandthebook.com

"Shortly after I opened Beauty and the Book, I founded The Pulpwood Queens of East Texas Book Club. I always wanted to be in a book club. Most of the book clubs that I had spoken to or visited as a guest, I found pretentious, stuffy, and more than a little like HOMEWORK! I decided if I ever wanted to be in a book club that I dreamed of, I would just have to start one, so I did!

"I told all of my clients and friends to come to my shop and we had six brave souls venture to the first meeting. I told the group that we were going to read a book a month, meet on the second Tuesday evening of each month, and we would all wear tiaras. They looked at me like deer caught in headlights! I kept plying them more wine, cheese, and crackers, and continued announcing that our motto was going to be 'where tiaras are mandatory and reading good books is the RULE!'

"Thanks to *Good Morning America*, we were featured kicking off their 'Read This!' Book Club, which has made us famous or maybe infamous. We now have over thirty chapters and are growing in leaps and bounds. Unless I'm told otherwise, I do believe we now have the largest 'meeting and discussing' book club in America, getting close to a thousand strong, and are proud promoters of literacy. We are running from Myrtle Beach, South Carolina, to Los Angeles, California. We even have chapters now run by men, yes, which we call our Timber Guys!

"Reading is a win, win, WIN situation and, to me, a book is the ultimate vacation from life. Believe you me with us all working like crazy; running our households, car-pooling the children, we need a much deserved and needed break! So grab a tiara and let's get READING!"

—Kathy Patrick

RED HAT SOCIETY

www.redhatsociety.com

"Where there is fun after fifty (and before) for women of all walks of life. We believe silliness is the comedy relief of life and, since we are all in it together, we might as well join red-gloved hands and go for the gusto together."

INDEX

A

Absences, 47, 49, 62
Accountability, 98, 100
Activist groups, 162–63
  field trips for, 109
  guest speakers for, 116
  handouts for, 75
  party favors for, 86
Advertising, 142
Agendas, 51–52, 100
Alcohol:
  for events at restaurants
    or bars, 127–28, 130,
    131–32
  hangover prevention and,
    80
  stressed member and, 96
Alexander, Zoe, 43, 54, 97,
    121–22, 126, 127, 129,
    135–36, 140
All-American Picnic theme,
  73
Application fees, 123
Applications, 122–25
Art groups, 136–37
  ideas for gatherings of,
    156
  retreats for, 110–11
  see also Culture clubs
Art Night, 40, 52, 79,
    110–11, 112–13
Ashare, Jennifer, 53, 127,
    128–29, 130–33, 140
Ask the Expert meetings,
  160
Attendance, rules on, 47,
    49, 62
Attrition, 49

B

Bank accounts, 61
Bars. See Restaurants or
  bars, meetings at
Beach Blankets? Bingo!
  theme, 73

Beading. See Craft circles
Beverages, 77, 78–79, 96
  alcoholic, for events at
    restaurants or bars,
    127–28, 130, 131–32
  hangover prevention and,
    80
  spiked punch, 78–79
Bible-study groups, 33, 40,
  96
  see also Hamlin, Carol;
    Spiritual gatherings
Bingo. See Gaming groups
Bird-watching. See Interest
  clubs
Board-game Pajama Party,
  158
Board games. See Gaming
  groups
Body Clinic theme, 162
Book clubs, 21, 62, 68,
  150–54
  field trips for, 108
  guest speakers for, 115
  handcrafted journal
    workshop for, 151
  handouts for, 74, 75
  large, breaking into
    smaller groups for
    discussion, 125–26
  party favors for, 85
  picking books for, 152
  playlists for, 81–82
  reading suggestions for
    (list), 152–54
  refreshments for, 76
  theme nights for, 73–74,
    151
  see also Pulpwood Queens
Brainstorming Barnstormer
  theme, 159
Branches, franchising and,
  143–46
Breakfast meetings, 131
Brown-bag It lunch, 157
Browne, Stephanie, 38
Buddhism. See Spiritual
  gatherings

Budgets:
  for girl groups, 32, 60
  see also Financial clubs
Bush, George W., 16

C

Candle making. *See* Craft
  circles
Cards. *See* Gaming groups
Career clubs, 156–57
  field trips for, 109
  guest speakers for, 115
  handouts for, 75
  party favors for, 86
Car-rental guidelines, 108
Casino outings. *See* Gaming
  groups
Casino Royale theme, 158
Cell phones, 50, 62
Charades, 117
Check requests, 99
Chill Out playlist, 81
Cinema Passionada theme,
  160
Cliques, 95
Club Jeopardy game, 117
Color, signature, 136
Color Clinic theme, 159
Conference calls, 44
Conversation Starters, 117
Cooking clubs, 76
  handouts for, 75
  playlists for, 82–84
Cooper, Sue Ellen, 58
Craft circles, 158–60
  field trips for, 109–10
  guest speakers for, 115
  handouts for, 74, 75
  party favors for, 86
  playlists for, 81–82
  refreshments for, 76
Cranes Fly for Peace, 16
Crochet, 13
  see also Craft circles
Crossley, Callie, 16, 74, 97
Culture clubs, 154–56
  field trips for, 108–9
  guest speakers for, 115

handouts for, 75
party favors for, 86
Cycling clubs, 74, 113
see also Sporting clubs

D

Decision-making, 50, 54–55
Decor, 68–74
indoor, themes for, 68–73
for meetings at restaurants
or bars, 132
outdoor, themes for, 73–74
Delegation, 52–53, 94, 95,
100
Depression, 92–93, 96
Dinner, hosting and, 59–60,
76–77
Dinner groups, 14–15, 26,
68
see also Divas Uncorked™
Disagreements:
feuding and, 93–94
mutual respect and, 50
resolving, 54–55
Disciplinary action, 62–63
Disinterested members,
94–95
Dislike for other member, 93
Divas Uncorked™, 16, 26,
38, 59–60, 66, 74, 79,
80, 91, 97, 99–100,
110, 138, 143, 168
Divas Who Dine, 33, 43,
58–59, 97, 121–22,
126–27, 128–29,
135–36, 140, 142–43,
145, 168
Divination groups, 68
see also Spiritual gatherings
Division of labor, 52–53, 111
Dogs Are Barking theme,
165–66
Domain names, 133
Domineering members, 94
Downers affecting group or
individual members,
106
Dream Team theme, 163

Dues, 47, 50, 60, 98, 123

E

e Bond, 40, 44, 52, 79,
110–11, 112–13
Educational handouts, 74
EIN numbers, 141
Elections, 53–54
E-mail:
extending invitations by,
42
for meeting reminders, 49
Emotional support groups,
162–63
field trips for, 109
guest speakers for, 116
handouts for, 75
party favors for, 86
Entertainment, 80–85
see also Guest speakers;
Playlists
Essays, for prospective
members, 123
Events:
field trips, 106–10
guest speakers, 84–85,
113–16
holiday parties, 112–13
meetings at restaurants or
bars, 86, 126–33
retreats, 110–12, 161
Evites, 41–42
Existing group, joining,
34–35, 168
Expenses, 26, 27
budgeting of, 32

F

Feuding, 93–94
Field trips, 106–10
club-specific ideas for,
108–9
transportation to, 107–8
Fifties theme, 69–72
Film Festival theme, 155
Financial clubs, 149–50
field trips for, 108
guest speakers for, 115

handouts for, 74
party favors for, 85
playlists for, 81–82
Fish-house Punch, 78
Focus level, 23
Franchising, 143–46
Fun activities, 116–17
Fund-raisers, 60, 118

G

Gambling. See Gaming
groups
Game Grab Bag, 158
Gaming groups, 157–58
field trips for, 109
guest speakers for, 115
handouts for, 74, 75
party favors for, 86
playlists for, 82–84
refreshments for, 76
structure for talk times
in, 56
themes for meetings of, 72,
158
Girl Power playlist, 83
Goals for group, 56–59
Goddess Within theme, 164
Goins, Liesa, 118
Good Old Girls' Night,
156–57
Greed Is Good theme, 150
Group dynamics, 37
Guest speakers, 84–85,
113–16
club-specific ideas for,
115–16
fees for, 114
finding, 113–14

H

Hamlin, Carol, 15, 33, 40,
48, 49, 63, 69–72,
90–91, 93, 96, 111, 112
Handouts, 74–76, 84
Handwritten invitations, 41
Hangover prevention, 80
Heat It Up playlist, 83–84
Hiking clubs, 30–32, 109,

122, 135, 136
see also Sporting clubs
Holidays:
helping families in need
at, 118
parties for, 112–13
Hosting, 65–86
assessing your space for,
66, 67–68
decor and, 68–74
entertainment and, 80–85
ground rules for, 59–60
guests and, 84–85
handouts and, 74–76, 84
lighting and, 68
party favors and, 85–86
refreshments and, 59, 60,
76–80
at restaurant or bar, 86,
126–33
seating and, 67–68
Howard, Donna, 14–15, 48

I
Image, maintaining
consistency in, 135–37
Incorporation, 140–41
Indoor decor, themes for,
68–73
Interest clubs, 160–61
field trips for, 109
guest speakers for, 115
handouts for, 75
party favors for, 86
Interrupting, 50, 55, 62,
89–90
Interviews, of prospective
members, 122
Introductions, starting
meetings with, 129–30
Investment clubs, 14, 40,
56, 68, 122
see also Financial clubs
Invitations to join group,
41–44

J
Jewelry making. *See* Craft

circles
Joining existing group,
34–35, 168
Jones, Pete, 140, 142
Journals:
handcrafting, 151
keeping in touch with
members who move or
travel through, 44
see also Craft circles

K
Kabbalah. See Spiritual
gatherings
Kicking someone out, 101–2
Kids, 50
Knitting circles, 13, 68, 76
see also Craft circles
Knock Three Times, 14–15,
48

L
Ladies Lodge theme, 68–69
Ladies Who Lunch theme,
69–72
Lady Luck Night theme, 72
Lande, Debra, 15, 37, 48,
55–56, 76–77, 92, 111
Lateness, 47, 49, 62, 91–92
Letterhead, 136, 137
Life coaching. *See* Career
clubs
Lighting, 68
Locations for meetings, 24
see also Restaurants or
bars, meetings at
Logos, 136, 137
Luau—Aloha! theme, 73
Luncheons, Sandwich Loaf
for, 70–72
Lunch groups:
fifties theme for, 69–72
see also Divas Who Dine
Lunch meetings, for career
groups, 157

M
Mah-jongg groups, 37,

55–56, 111
see also Gaming groups;
Lande, Debra
Male bashing, 16, 50
Mardi Gras theme, 69
Meditation. *see also* Spiritual
gatherings
Meetings:
agendas for, 51–52
breakfast, 131
decor for, 68–74, 132
frequency of, 24, 27
fun activities for, 116–17
handouts for, 74–76, 84
introductions at start of,
129–30
lighting for, 68
men at, 16, 50
music for, 80–84
party favors for, 85–86,
132
punctuality and
attendance rules for,
47, 49
refreshments for, 50, 59,
60, 76–80
at restaurants or bars, 86,
126–33
scheduling of, 24, 26,
48–49
special guests or speakers
at, 84–85, 113–16
venues for, 24, 27, 65–68
Members, problematic
behaviors of, 89–102
chronic lateness, 47, 49,
62, 91–92
disinterest, 94–95
dislike for one another,
43, 93–94
domineering behavior, 94
dropping the ball, 98
feeling shunned or left
out, 95–96
kicking someone out due
to, 101–2
money-related, 98–99
motormouths, 90–91

negativity or depression,
92–93, 96
obnoxious behavior,
89–90, 97
pushing own agenda or
business, 97
rigidity about rules and
procedures, 96
socializing outside of
group, 101
splintering into cliques,
95
stress-related, 96
talking over one, 91
type-A personalities and,
99–100
type-B personalities and,
100
Membership, 21–22, 28–32,
37–40, 122–26
ability to share
responsibilities and, 40
applications and
interviews for, 122–25
attrition and, 49
creating level playing
field and, 26
dealing with friends not
chosen and, 37–38
duties or responsibilities
required for, 125–26
extending invitation for,
41–44
flowcharts with critical
criteria and, 30–32
friends in far-flung
locales and, 44
group dynamics and, 37
groups evolved from
other entities and, 38–40
heading off potential
problems and, 21–22
ideal mix and, 40
ideal qualities and, 28, 38
personality assessment
and, 38, 39
second round of
invitations and, 42–43

size of group and, 14, 27,
41, 43–44, 121–22
on trial basis, 122
Venn diagrams for
compatibility and,
28–30
Men, at gatherings, 16, 50
Mentor Mixer, 157
Mission statements, 56–59
Mixing it up, 116–17
Mocha Moms, 168–69
Mocha Moms L.A., 48, 59,
60–61, 90, 93–94, 97,
98, 105, 123–25, 138,
168
Modus operandi, 22–23, 25
Money issues, 59–61, 98–99
bank accounts, 61
budgets, 32, 60
check requests, 99
in choosing potential
members, 26
dues, 47, 50, 60, 98, 123
hostessing costs, 59–60
monitoring of funds,
60–61
Monopoly Night, 150
Mothers groups, 139
see also Mocha Moms
Motormouths, 90–91
Movie clubs, 14, 40, 62, 67,
68, 113
Film Festival theme and,
155
handouts for, 74, 75
Oscar night gatherings
for, 154–55
refreshments for, 73–74,
76
theme nights for, 73–74
see also Culture clubs
Movies:
for craft circles, 159
for interest clubs, 160
Music:
playlists for meetings,
80–84
recitals, 155

sing-alongs, 164–65
see also Culture clubs

N
Name of group, 33
incorporation and, 140
trademarking, 142
National Mah-jongg
League (NMJL),
55–56
Needlepoint. See Craft circles
Negative emotions, 92–93,
100
Networking. See Career
clubs
Newsletters, 137–38

O
Obnoxious behavior, 89–91,
97
Oscar night gatherings,
154–55
Outdoor decor, themes for,
73–74

P
Pageant Prizes, 162
Painting Party, 156
Pajama parties, 73, 158
Party favors, 85–86, 132
Passport Party, 156
Patrick, Kathy, 13–14, 15,
118, 125–26, 143, 145,
151–52, 169–70
Peace organizations, 16
Personality traits, 25, 112
Petrie, Sherry, 48, 59, 90,
93–94, 97, 98, 123–25,
138
Pets, 50
Philanthropic activity, 118
Phone calls:
cell phones and, 50, 62
conference calls, 44
extending invitations by,
42
Photos of members and
events, 136

Picnics, 73
Playdate, 163
Playlists, 80–84
energy, 82–84
mellow, 81–82
Poetry, 155
see also Culture clubs
Poker nights, 13, 68, 74, 76
see also Gaming groups
Potlucks, 79–80
Press kits, 41, 142
Printed materials, 135–37
maintaining consistent
image in, 135–37
newsletters, 137–38
Promotion, 138–40
maintaining consistent i
mage in, 135–37
Web sites and, 133–35
Pulpwood Queens, 33,
55, 58, 118, 125–26,
139, 143, 145, 151–52,
169–70
Punch, spiked, 78–79
Punctuality, rules on, 47,
49, 62

Q
Q&A game, 116
Quilting circles, 76, 135, 136
see also Craft circles
Quiz Show, 117

R
Rabble rousing, 163
Recitals, 155
Red Hat Society, 55, 58, 170
Refreshments, 50, 76–80
activities during meeting
and, 76
easy to make and neat to
eat, 77–78
money issues and, 59, 60
potlucks, 79–80
special dietary needs and,
76
see also Beverages
Resources, 168–70

Respect, mutual, 49–50
Restaurants or bars,
meetings at, 86, 126–33
alcohol for, 127–28, 130,
131–32
menu for, 127–28
negotiating price for,
128–29
private rooms and space
arrangements for, 129
scheduling and booking,
130–32
Retreats, 110–12, 161
Rigidity, 96
Rock Out playlist, 84
Rules and guidelines, 47–63
for admission to group,
122–25
agendas and, 51–52
for decision-making, 50,
54–55
for delegation and
division of labor, 52–53
for disciplinary action,
62–63
for elections, 53–54
for festive and fun
elements, 55
ground, suggested, 50
importance of, 47–48
for maintaining
membership, 125–26
money issues and, 59–61
for pulling equal weight,
50
for punctuality and
attendance, 47, 49, 62
referring to other clubs or
organizations for, 55–56
rigidity about, 96
rules of conduct, 49–50,
61–63
for scheduling, 48–49
Running groups, 21
see also Sporting groups

S
Safety Dance theme, 162

Sandwich Loaf, 70–72
Schedule:
of group meetings, 24, 26,
48–49
personal, 24, 25, 26
Scholarship funds, 118
Scrapbooking. *See* Craft
circles
Seating, for gatherings,
67–68, 95
Seeing Red theme, 162
Self-awareness exercises,
22–26
Sing-alongs, 164–65
Size of group, 14, 27, 41,
43–44, 66
growing pains and,
121–22
Slumber Party theme, 73
Social comfort level, 23, 25
Socializing outside of
group, 101
Spa Exotic theme, 166
Spa parties, 165–66
field trips for, 109
guest speakers for, 116
handouts for, 75–76
party favors for, 86
playlists for, 81–82
Zen Den theme for, 69
Speakers. *See* Guest speakers
Speaking:
guidelines for, 50, 62
interrupting and, 50, 55,
62, 89–90
motormouths and, 90–91
talking over one another
and, 91
Spin the Bottle, 116
Spiritual gatherings, 164–65
field trips for, 109
guest speakers for, 116
handouts for, 75
party favors for, 86
Sponsors, 142–43
Sporting clubs, 161–62
field trips for, 109
guest speakers for, 115

handouts for, 74, 75
party favors for, 86
Spreadsheets, 60
Starting a girl group:
    budgeting, 32
    choosing women to
        invite, 21–22, 28–32,
        37–40. See also
        Membership
    drafting statement of
    goals or mission
        statement, 56–59
    extending invitations,
        41–44
    naming group, 33
    particulars for planning
        stage of, 26–28
    self-awareness exercises
        and, 22–26
Stitch 'n' bitch nights, 13
Stressed members, 96
Summer Solstice, 164
Swing Out, Sister! playlist,
    82

T
Talk times, structure for, 56
Tardiness, 47, 49, 62, 91–92
Tea, afternoon, 77
Theater clubs. see Culture
    clubs
Theme gatherings, 73–74,
    151
Time management, 51
Trademarking your name,
    142
Transportation, for field
    trips, 107–8
Travel. See Interest clubs
Triangulation, 101
Trust, 62
Truth or Dare, 116
TV clubs. See Culture clubs
Type-A personalities,
    99–100
Type-B personalities, 100

V
Veg Out playlist, 81–82
Venn diagrams, 28–30
Venues for meetings, 24, 27,
    65–68
    see also Restaurants or bars,
        meetings at
Von Arx, Jared, 79

W
Web sites, 133–35
    maintaining consistent
    image in, 135–37
Wharton, Jo, 13, 16, 38, 48,
    56
Wicca. See Spiritual
    gatherings
Wine clubs, 26, 68
    See also Divas
        Uncorked™; Interest
        groups
Woo Woo Women theme,
    165
Writing. See Interest clubs

Y
Yahoo! groups, 44
Young, Maria, 48, 49,
    91–92, 139

Z
Zen Den theme, 69